INFINITE REPETITION
IN A FINITE WORLD

INFINITE REPETITION

IN A FINITE WORLD

Four Snapshots of:
Love, Self, Mind, God, and the Universe.
Plus, a Dust of Imagination!

Marlene N. Seara, MSW

DISCLAIMER

The interpretations and opinions expressed in this book, particularly in the essay titled *"Snap Shot of God and the Universe,"* are solely those of the author. The creation story and the nature of space is not intended to be presented as factual or scientifically proven. These ideas are derived from the author's intuition and vivid imagination.

The author's intent is to share an alternative perspective and provide insights into various aspects of life, including love, self, and the mind. Readers who choose to engage with any of the practices or concepts described in this book do so at their own discretion. Neither the author nor the publisher accepts any responsibility or liability for any outcomes resulting from the use of the content provided.

Library of Congress
ISBN:
Paperback: 979-8-90190-122-9
Hardcover: 979-8-90190-123-6

Acknowledgment

Heartfelt thanks to my family and dear friends. Your honest feedback in the early stages—when my book was a mix of genres without a clear direction—became a turning point. Your voices stayed with me through the years, shaping this journey. I am deeply grateful!

A special thanks goes to Karen, my sister-in-law, my cousin Zoraida, and her children, Zorylena and Pedrito, all who leapt in and rescued me when I needed it most. Your support during the final edits helped carry me to the finish line. Your belief made all the difference.

Preface

Writing this book has been a long and evolving journey—over fifteen years in the making. It began as a creative project, a collection of poems/prose, quotes, and short stories written purely for the joy of expression. In its early days, I envisioned its title as *Words, Thoughts, and Dreams*. But as the writing deepened, the title transformed, changing many times as the content took shape.

At one point, I had written 35 poems/prose pieces, but no essays yet. Unsure whether poetry/prose still had an audience, I visited a Barnes & Noble to browse the poetry/prose section—only to find it nearly empty. It was not a promising sign. Disheartened but still hopeful, I sought feedback from friends and family. By then, my writing had expanded to include essays, short stories, and quotations. Their responses were honest: too many ideas, too much content, and no clear structure.

That feedback became a turning point. After much reflection, I restructured the book into its current form—a focused, cohesive exploration of four themes: **Love, Self, Mind, and God**. Over the years, I refined its structure, clarified its themes, and made thoughtful revisions. What began as a creative outlet eventually became a personal mission.

In 2025, I made a resolution: to finish and publish this book. And now, here it is in your hands—a humble offering of thoughts on four essential aspects of life: Love, Self, Mind, God, and the Universe — woven together with curiosity, intuition, insight, and imagination.

By nature, I am an optimist. I believe in the power of reflection and the quiet wisdom found in life's everyday moments. My hope is that this book encourages you to explore your own relationship with love, identity, emotions, reactions, and your understanding of the divine.

I believe God is a deeply personal experience, one that speaks to each of us in different ways. As you read, I invite you to embrace what I call the three "I's": **Intuition, Insight, and Imagination**.

Peace, Love, and Goodwill to All.

Introduction

What does it mean to exist—truly and fully—in this finite world?

In Infinite Repetition in a Finite World, I explore the universal themes of four fundamental aspects of life: **Love, Self, Mind, and God**—and, by extension, the Universe. Each essay is accompanied by a prose piece that reflects on the same themes.

As a first-time author, initially, I wrote a series of poems/prose grouped into those four themes. The first three essays evolved into self-reflective, personal-growth essays rooted in my personal experiences as a social worker and infused with my own interpretations. The fourth essay—on **God, the Universe, and the origins of space before and after the Big Bang**—took more than a decade to complete.

I immersed myself in research for that final essay, exploring religion, philosophy, metaphysics, chemistry, mathematics, and cosmology. At times, I paused my writing for weeks, allowing ideas to percolate before returning with fresh insight. The process of exploring God became a journey, each page a step toward understanding.

My intention is to invite you, the reader, to consciously reflect on the interconnectedness of these universal ideas. To pause, to look inward, and to consider your own beliefs, thought patterns, and possibilities. I hope this book resonates with the part of you that seeks clarity, beauty, and a deeper sense of existence.

Marlene N. Seara, MSW

July 2025

Table of Contents

ESSAY #1

Snapshot of Love

An Interpretation of the Power of Love

There are two risks worth taking—one in love and one in life itself, and both are worth the risk.

Snapshot of Love

An Interpretation of the Power of Love

What is Love?

The misunderstanding about love often begins when we ask the question: What is love? Subconsciously, we immortalize love through literature, poetry, and art. Consciously, we manifest love in romantic relationships, acts of care, and service to others. Love is both a deeply personal experience and a universal force that binds us all.

Throughout history, love has been defined in many ways, each offering a unique perspective. In my view, love is a **Universal-Life-Force** with three main manifestations:

1. Love as the First Expression of Life
2. Love Yourself and Share Your Love with Others
3. Universal Love

MANIFESTATION #1:

Love as the First Expression of Life

I see love and life as two sides of the same coin, interconnected and inseparable. Life cannot flourish without love, and love cannot exist without life. When we understand this truth, we reconnect with the universal life-force that sustains all existence.

In this interpretation, the universal life-force may be called *God or a Supreme Being*. However, if that term does not resonate immediately, do not worry, the universal life-force meets us wherever we are in our personal and spiritual journey. By spiritual, I mean the energy that gives life, not necessarily religious belief.

This manifestation includes three subconscious perceptions:

1. Recognition of a Universal Life-Force
2. Awareness that We Are Creators
3. Love Requires Respect Life

1. First Subconscious Perception: Recognizing the Universal Life-Force

Since ancient times, humanity has observed an intelligent force in nature. The rhythm of the seasons, the ocean's tides, the splendor of the mountains, and the miracle of birth. Ancient civilizations, from Egypt to Greece, perceived this force as divine, giving it names such as Ra, Zeus, and Apollo.

Yet the word God can be misused when employed for control or manipulated for personal or societal control. Here, I define God as **an Intelligent Life-Force,** an energy present in nature, the cosmos, and within ourselves. Physically, we are made of the same chemical elements as the stars. Spiritually, we are one with all existence.

2. Second Subconscious Perception: Awareness that We Are Creators!

We as humans have an extraordinary ability to reinvent ourselves. We are thinkers, builders, dreamers, and innovators. We are not bound by circumstances; we have the power to transform our lives. To consciously recognizing this potential enables us to shape our lives according to our highest aspirations.

To initiate change, we must first become conscious of our thought's patterns. Our subconscious mind holds our habits, beliefs, and fears. But it also contains the raw material for transformation. Once we consciously understand that we have control over our thoughts, we can begin to shape our lives with purpose.

Key Messages:

- Consciously recognize that we are Creators.
- Consciously recognize that we have the power to transform our lives.
- Our task is to convert subconscious perception into "conscious realities."
- To choose is our privilege.

3. Third Subconscious Perception: Love Requires Respect for Life

This subconscious perception begins as a whisper of love and grows louder with awareness.

Love is shown through how we respect life in all its forms: human, animal, plant, and environment. Even if you struggle to feel universal love, start with respect.

Respect Life:

- Self: Value your own existence.
- Animals: Do not harm them for pleasure. Show compassion.
- People: Respect cultural, religious, and moral differences. Avoid using words like weapons.
- Environment: Reduce pollution. Conserve resources, and acknowledge climate changes.

In my view, older generations are having a hard time acknowledging climate change. Perhaps, this perception may still have a dormant environmental awareness in them. My intuition tells me that new generations are born with an *instinct* instead of a *subconscious* perception.

New generations carry this consciousness as instinct. They are born with a deep concern for the Earth and its well-being.

MANIFESTATION #2: Love Yourself and Share Your Love with Others

To love oneself is not **Narcissistic** it is foundational. Before we can give or receive love, we must recognize our own worth.

What Does It Mean to Love Yourself?

- Recognize your uniqueness and purpose.
- Being authentic and embracing your strengths and flaws.
- Rise above challenges and honor your self-worth.

Self-love is not indulgence; it is the path to self-awareness. Only then can we share love authentically with others.

Sharing Love with Others

The hallmark of love is *giving*. Each interaction, personal, professional, or social is an opportunity to grow. Helping others deepens our capacity to love. However, to truly share love, we must clear obstacles like *negativity* and *resentment*.

How to Eliminate Negativity

- Do not dwell on negative thoughts, acknowledge them, and move on.
- Replace them with uplifting actions: walk, dance, listen to music, engage in a hobby.

Thoughts and feelings are linked. All feelings echo our thoughts. Intention gives thoughts their direction and purpose. This is why it is important to know what we are thinking. If we consciously know what we think, we can trace our emotions and actions back to their root. Our behavior is a side effect of what we think. *If you do not like your behavior, change your thinking.*

The question is, how can one eliminate negative thoughts? It is very simple. However, it requires a lot of work and effort on your part. What you need to do is choose to start today by doing the following:

A Simple Method for Replacing Negative Thoughts:

1. Let the negative thought come. Acknowledge it and MOVE ON.
2. When the negative thought comes, make believe that you are watching TV if you do not like the program. (thought) "Change the channel, Change the Thought"
3. Do something else immediately. By doing this, your intentions also change. Repeat 1 and 2 until you win the battle.
4. Use a reminder sign:

I CAN DO IT!

MOVE ON

I AM DESIGNING MY NEW LIFE

If you prefer, add a picture of yourself moving, and put the sign in a visible place where you can see it often. *To Move On* is the first step. The second step is to *Consciously Acknowledge* what you think and then say to yourself:

I DO NOT ALLOW _____ (insert the negative thought or emotion) to enter my life. **It has no power over me.** IT HAS NO POWER OVER ME! Repeat this until it becomes your reality.

Refocus your attention on converting negative thinking into positive actions. Simply switch your concentration of negative thoughts to positive actions. Do one negative thought at a time.

You must replace the negative thought with action. The action can be to go out for a walk, dance, or do anything that the reader enjoys.

You must do this switching exercise every time a negative thought appears. Be patient and just do it until one day Eureka! Remember Do Not Quit! Do Not Quit .....the victory will be yours!

Five Tips to Overcome Negativity:

1. Have the desire to change the negative attitude or thought."
2. Cultivate Self-discipline.
3. Use willpower to persevere. Never quit, regardless of daily challenges.
4. Persist one day at a time.
5. Never Quit! Start all over again if needed.

Use reminders from people you admire. For me, Abraham Lincoln is a model. He failed 16 times before becoming president of the United States of America. You can find someone that you admire or respect and use it as a reminder note, *"To Never, Never Quit." If that does not work. I read the "Serenity Prayer."*

How to Eliminate a Negative Attitude:

To help you with this process, do the following every time you think that you have an attitude (Self-awareness is the key).

1. Consciously become aware of your gestures.
2. Consciously become aware of your breathing.
3. Consciously listen to the tone of your voice.
4. Observe how people react to you.
5. Listen to your own voice inside your head. (Self-talking)

Learn to recognize your "Attitude Traits." Consciously know them. You must *Recognize and Acknowledge* your actions. Otherwise, you will do things automatically, without thinking. See your reminder note as often as you can. Say the affirmation with conviction, followed by action. Affirmations must be followed by Actions, or it *does not work*. For positive affirmations, breathing and relaxation exercises, see Appendix A and B.

Repeat the exercises until negativity no longer dominates. Once that happens, you are ready to give love freely without self-interest. When one feels love, there is no room for self-interest behavior. Do not worry about receiving love. It will come back to you.

MANIFESTATION #3: Universal Love

Universal Love is unconditional. It is the conscious realization that we are both physical, the "I", and spiritual, the "I AM" beings. As we grow, we transcend the barriers of the ego (the "I") and recognize our oneness with all life.

At some point in our lives, we exceed the fence of the "I" and begin to awaken in our consciousness the Universal Love. When this awareness awakens, it becomes the foundation for true self-knowledge.

Throughout these four essays, the reader will have an insight into the authentic self.

The "I AM" and our connection with all life.

Formula: Love Yourself + Share Your Love=Power of Love

Interpretation Of Romantic Love

Breaking the False Idea of Romantic Love

Romantic love is often misunderstood when associated with jealousy, guilt, or resentment. These emotions distort love and create a dysfunctional relationship.

True love does not foster possessiveness or control. It seeks mutual growth and deep connection.

Love simply is! It can only be expressed through loving actions. Sometimes we wonder why romantic love does not last longer. Romantic love, in its early stages, is exhilarating, but to sustain it requires work, patience, and understanding.

When love begins to fade, couples must consciously work to reignite their bond. *Love is a partnership, not just an emotion.*

To love daily requires a lot of work, patience, and commitment. When one reaches the low curve of love, this means that "Action" is needed with the intention to recapture the old excitement of the first phase of love. We have two options:

1) Therapy, one-to-one. (If it is not too expensive.) Or,

2) Self-help books.

If you feel that you are at the curve of love, you may try the "Rescue Me Plan."

The "Rescue Me" Plan for Relationships:

ACTION #1: The Thinking Process

Think of the low curve of love as a signal of "Rescue Me." Now is the time to refocus your attention on your husband, wife, or significant other. Begin to examine your emotions.

The first question that you should ask yourself is. What does love mean to you? What actions make you feel loved?

Reflect on your Needs: Do not assume that your husband, wife, or even lover knows what your needs are. It is a must that you communicate your needs to your other half. Since a relationship is a partnership, both parties must agree to compromise. If he or she is not willing or cannot do it, then it is time for him or her to make a choice based on two factors.

1. How important is it for you to meet that need? Can you live without it? Can you be happy or content?

2. We must realize that people come into our lives with a history of good and bad habits. Frequently, we think that people will change; unfortunately, this hope is a fantasy. People can modify their behavior if and only if they are conscious of their actions, and they are willing to change on behalf of "the relationship" and accept responsibility for their mistakes.

Now, having those two factors in mind, let us proceed. Can you substitute some of your needs? If it is so, negotiate with your husband/wife/partner. Here is another issue to consider. What is more important to you in the relationship?

It can be honesty, trust, faithfulness, attention to detail, etc. Whatever it is for you, it must balance the total dimension of the relationship. Please take a moment and respond to the above questions. Write down the answers.

The most important thing is to ACT and DO SOMETHING about the relationship. If you do not deal with your needs now, eventually the relationship deteriorates and collapses. At the end, not only you, but everybody around you, feels miserable.

ACTION #2: Evaluate Your Emotions

Identify the positives and negatives in your relationship. Find a place where you cannot be interrupted. This action involves time to think and time to analyze your own emotions. After this analysis is done, write a list of those feelings. Then ask yourself the following two questions:

1. How many positive emotions are gone or decreased?

2. How many positive emotions are still there, or have increased?

Take two pages: On page 1, make 4 columns. (See Appendix C)

In column 1. Write this question: What positive emotions have decreased or are gone over the years?

In column 2. Write this question: What positive emotions have stayed or increased over time?

In column 3. Write this question. Why and what contributed to the failure?

For example, your partner used to give you a special gift for holidays or special occasions, but it does not happen anymore. This action was present in the first stage of love, but it is not present now.

You need to write all the excuses that he or she gave you. This is, of course, if you are still working on keeping the relationship, and you still have that need.

The opposite should be that he or she still gives you the same gift, or maybe new gifts. This is what you write in column 2. This column is to acknowledge loving acts.

In column 4, write this question. What happened to cause the decrease in loving acts?

Apply these questions to each of your answers in column 1.

Answer one question at a time. Do not analyze your response. Write what comes to mind.

ACTION #3: My Action Plan (I am my therapist, this is your page.)

After you finish with the 4 columns, put the paper away for a couple of hours, or until the next day, then go to the next step.

The second page is for you. Now you need to come up with an action plan. You are the best Therapist! This is your challenge!

Write the plan in detail. Write a to-do list. Be specific. Give yourself a time frame. Each partner will also include a Commitment Pledge. Do not waste more time! Do IT Now!

The "Rescue Me" Plan will give you:

- An understanding of what is going on in your relationship.

- You will know why your emotions increased or decreased.

- You will consciously understand that keeping a relationship involves a lot of work and commitment.

- Ask yourself why I chose this relationship instead of

  _____(fill the blank)

- You do not need to stay in a relationship if you do not really want it. However, if there are "forces" (children) that make you stay in the relationship, ask yourself this question. What do I need to learn from this relationship?

- Ask the question until you get an answer. Believe it or not, the answer will give you an opportunity to choose, and perhaps a possibility that it might change your life's situation. Just try it!

- The reason that you are working in this relationship is that you chose to do so. You still love your other half, and he or she is worth the effort. Measure the positive against the negative traits. The key phrase here is "If he or she is worthy?"

- Communicate with your partner and commit to growth. A relationship is like a garden; it requires constant care. If both partners are willing, love can flourish once again. If not, separate, and start all over again!

> # Good Luck! You Can Do It!
> # Start Now!

Essay Summary

Love is a universal force with three subconscious manifestations:

1. **Manifestation #1** covers 3 subconscious perceptions: **Recognition of a Universal Life force.** – Recognizing the life-force that connects us to all things. The Human Spirit.

2. The second perception: **The Awareness that we are Creators.** – We are not limited by life's events. We are thinker beings with the power to change our reality.

3. The third perception: **The Understanding that Love Requires Respect for life** – Respect begins with ourselves, then respect for everything else, animals, plants, etc. Understanding these connections brings us to unconditional love.

Manifestation #2: Love Yourself and Share Your Love with Others. This manifestation talks about how important it is to learn how to love yourself. After learning how to love yourself, the next step is to share your love with others.

Manifestation#3 Universal Love is the conscious realization that we are both physical, the "I", and spiritual beings, the "I AM". This recognition brings our humanity in us and our unconditional love for everything that exists.

It is followed by an interpretation of Romantic Love. It includes an action plan and gives the reader ideas of how to rescue the old flame.

Key Message:

Love is not just an emotion; it is an action and a commitment. By awakening these subconscious perceptions, we empower ourselves to live fully, love deeply, and contribute to a more compassionate world.

In the next essay, you will learn what your authentic self is.

BONUS

PROSE
OF
LOVE

Sketches of Love

1
Falling in love is not true love.
True love begins when the magic fades.

2
The first phase of love
is the hardest to forget.

3
Love is growing together, emotionally.
Love is built on tolerance and commitment.

4
Love is a free choice of the mind.
Love is life in motion.

5
Staying in love takes constant effort.
To truly love is a work of art.

6
If you feel emotionally distant
from partner or lover—
It may be time to move on.

7
Love is working through the rough patches.
Love is discovering yourself through the other.

8
Love is a masterpiece of the heart and mind.
Love is the eternal flame of humanity.

Love Is Freedom

Love has no age.
Love has no race.

Love
Does not discriminate.

Poor, Rich, White, Black.
Young and Old.

Love is the attraction of two souls.
The affinity of two lives.

Love is a shared moment.
Love is a moment of silence.

Love is your thought.
Love is a fearless force.

Love is freedom.
I am free! You are free!

We choose!

The First Look

Just one look!
One contact!

The body trembles.
My eyes, your eyes.

Emotion of the senses.
Desire of the heart.

Impossible to sustain the look!
You captivated my soul.

Simultaneous attraction.
Where do you come from?

Centuries of seconds.
Travel through my body.

Stop looking!

Or the world will know
that in a split second.

I lost my soul!

Do Not Ignore Me

Do you think I can ignore you?

Can the waves ignore the ocean?
Can the fish ignore the water?

Can I, mortal of dreams and desires,
ignore your passion or ignore your love.

Do you think I can ignore you?

Can the painter overlook its subject?
Can nature turn back the season?

NO!
I cannot ignore you.

I am seduced!
In the web of your presence.

I am lost in the sound of your voice.

Can I, creature of emotions,
ignore your intoxicating feeling of love.

Do you think I can ignore you?

NO!
I cannot ignore you.

I am trapped!

The Pleasure of Love

The care, the love, the attention.
Happiness of two souls.
Enjoyment of two lives.

Pleasures of the senses.
Love is to live.
Exciting, delightful moments.
Amusing stories of the past.
Sometimes, love can be confusing.
Unpredictable, let us
Redefine love and rearrange life.
Enjoy the breeze of romance.

Once you love, you are contaminated.
Fog, haze, confusion.

Love is a gentle wind.
Once you love, you are infected!
Vaccines do not work.
Exaltation of love is the cure!

Love Is Gone

Love has faded away.
Shattered by time.
Once you awakened my passion.
Once you intoxicated my soul.
Once you were my love.

Love...
Where did you go?

The Fascination.
The Attraction.
The Madness.
The Magic.
The Spell.
Is gone!

Why did the mysteries disappear?
Love might not be real?

Divine illusion of the senses.
Love, where are you now?

Dust of Love

Destiny.
Passion.
Love.
Fate.

Take a deep breath and inhale.
The atom of life is around you.

Now, walk and review your life.
Find yourself. It is time to discover.

Who are you? What do you want?
Where would you like to be?

You are ready to search.
Nothing can stop you!

Just take a deep breath and inhale.
I am dust!

The master of time devoured my body.
And released my soul. I am everywhere!

Just take a deep breath and inhale.
Now, I am part of you. I am with you!

I am everywhere!
I am with you!

Love is a Bubble

We cross each other's paths.
You are there on Earth.
I am everywhere.

I am a thought!

Love is many things.
Do we understand love?
Or do we just perceive love?

Love is life in action!

Love is like a bubble.
You do not know that you are in it.
Until it breaks!

Silence!
Something is popping!

Who Is Looking for Love?

Maybe You.
Maybe Him.
Maybe Her.
Who knows?

Who wants to be loved?

Loves me, yes!
Loves me, not!
"Where is The Gardener?"
Asks the Yellow Rose.

I AM the gardener!
Whisper the wind to the rose.
Loves me, yes!
Loves me, not!

Love sleeps in each seed.
Love awakes in each flower.
Loves me yes, loves me not.
Who is looking for love?

It's all of us!

Loves me, yes!
Loves me not!
Loves me, yes!
Loves me, not!

Capsules of Love

1
Believes in love.
 Is not important.

2
What is important
Is what you do with love.

3
Love is not guilt.
Love is self-respect.

4
Love is not jealousy.
Love is trust.

5
Love is not possession.
Love is selflessness.

6
Trust real love.
Not its absence!

Romanticism

Romanticism, illusion of the heart.

One can crave it.

Many do not have the skills.

A skill one must develop.

New ways of feeling love.

Thousands of ways to say "I love you."

Insatiable desire of the heart.

Cause of much dissolution.

Is romanticism an art of the senses or,

Subconscious sketches of the mind or,

Myth or fable of love?

Love is a Process

Love smiles at you.
You smiled back!
What rules over love?

Is it the heart?
Is it the mind?
What goes first?

The heart.
The mind.
Who cares?

No matter who goes first.
You are a winner!

When love whispered to you.
You murmured back!

And
The process begins....

Love is Alive

Why does love crumble?
Your attitude.
My attitude.
Just words.
And interpretations.

Love is alive!

It changes over time.
Most difficult words.
Anger.
Jealousy.
Communication.
Guilt.
Ownership.
Resentment.

My truth, your truth.
Who is right?
Or
We just react.
Impulsively.
Passionately

Love is a changeable creature!
Real love begins.
When a relationship starts.

Perception of Love

Paradise of Dreams.
Ecstasy of the senses.
Reaction of the heart.
Creation of love.
Endless feelings of happiness.
Portrait of a dream.
Temptation of the soul.
Infatuation, impulse.
Obsession
Notion of life and pain.

Original desire.
Force of the universe.

Love and believe
One voice "I AM"
Vibration of sounds.
Endless music of love.

Dangerous Verb

*Your name is
synonymous with desire.
Your presence is
an adjective of love.*

*Dangerous verb.
I love.
You love.*

*I hear your voice.
I shake.
I see your face.
I am lost!*

*Passion is the subject.
Obsession is the noun.*

*Love is the Messenger.
Hide and seek is its code.*

*Love is a classical play.
History is the theater!*

*Action! Dangerous verb.
I love.
You love.
We play!*

Who Loves You Now?

Poetry.
Where did you go?

Did the culture leave you?
Or is poetry just gone?

Instead of poetry.
There is a school curriculum.

Culturally, we are changing!
Who loves poetry now?

Where is the passion?
Where is the romance?

Can a writer lift your spirit?
Can a poem seduce an audience?

Can we listen to the endless beat?
Of rhythm and sounds.

Love, Life, and Poetry
Change over time!

Poetry.
Where are you now?

I Love You As...

I love you.
...As the tree adores its leaves.

I adore you.
...As the leaves embrace the wind.

I embrace you.
...As the wind idolizes the air.

I idolize you.
...As the air glorifies the stars.

I need you.
...As the stars cannot live without the galaxy.

I miss you.
...As the galaxy cannot survive without gravity.

I hold you.
...As gravity filled the universe.

I worship you.
...As the universe gazes at creation.

This is love, a constant mixture of elements!
This is life, a constant action of love.

ESSAY   #2

Snapshot of Self

An Interpretation of You and Me

When you become consciously aware of yourself, you have taken the first step of self-discovery.

ESSAY

2

What is the Authentic Self?

The concept of the self is multifaceted in this exploration. I will focus on the duality of the self, the Conscious Self, and the Authentic Spiritual Self. These two aspects interpenetrate one another, creating a delicate balance between the "I" that is defined by perceptions, reactions, thoughts, and emotions.

The physical "I" exists in a temporary body. We qualify this "I" by saying: I am a teacher, a carpenter, a social worker, married, single, etc. These labels shift and change over time, but the Authentic Self remains. This "I AM" is an unqualified "I," the eternal and infinite part of us that is connected to the greater cosmic whole. This "I AM" is not defined by names or roles; it is simply the pure presence of being.

Our physical bodies serve as instruments, tools through which we experience life and fulfill our spiritual evolution. Though we each experience life differently, we all share the capacity to think, feel, and behave sometimes in harmony, other times in discord. Consciously, we recognize our bodies, our thoughts, and our emotions. But beneath that awareness, there is a subtle whisper, a quiet call urging us toward our Authentic Self.

This whisper may manifest as intuition, or perhaps as an insight that leads us to seek our true essence. Imagine that the Authentic/Spiritual Self is immortal. The Conscious Self is tied to the physical, mental, and emotional realms. The Conscious Self often reacts out of instinct, emotion, or circumstance. These two selves are in constant tension, and that conflict can only be resolved when we awaken to the truth of who we are…the Authentic Self.

We often ask: Who am I? What is my purpose in life? These are age-old questions, yet the answer lies in the quiet voice of our subconscious mind, urging us to rediscover the Authentic Self. The self we have forgotten. The Spiritual Self is eternal, invisible, and free of the fluctuations of the material world. Meanwhile, our physical bodies are but shells, changing with time. The body, however, is the vehicle that allows our spiritual journey to unfold; without it, there will be no spiritual evolution.

For centuries, we have grappled with the duality of our physical and spiritual selves. To recognize the spiritual self, we must consciously transcend the limitations of the physical. But How?

The Path of Self-Awareness

The first step is to consciously eliminate fear, negativity, and harmful intentions. These are the "barriers" that cloud our path. They manifest as fatigue, anxiety, depression, and illness. Clearing these obstacles clears the way for new awareness, one that opens us to new emotions like gratitude, empathy, and compassion.

Second, we must recognize that we are responsible for our actions and decisions. There are four key principles that help guide this process of self-discovery.

1   The Principle of Free Will
2   The Principle of Cause and Effect
3   The Principle of Karma
4   The Principle of Repetition - Habits

1. The Principle of Free Will

We are free to choose. Whether it is choosing the color of our clothes or deciding whether to think positively or negatively, our freedom defines who we are. This freedom comes with responsibility. We are accountable for our actions and reactions. No external forces, not even God, control our fate.

Free will is the blueprint of our existence. It provides the opportunity to learn from past mistakes in past lives or our current life, and to consciously shape our future. While life may present challenges, how we respond to them determines the trajectory of our spiritual evolution. Free will enables us to change course, to learn, and to evolve. To help you to understand this process. The principle of Cause and effect and Karma will answer some of your questions.

In my interpretation, the story of our physical self begins even before we are born. All of us decide what we call *"our destiny"*. Destiny is not an inevitable fate. Destiny is our design, a plan that we will use to overcome our past mistakes. Below is an example of choice.

I recall a recurring dream from my younger years, which vividly illustrates the power of choice. A young boy, about three years old, would ask me, repeatedly, to be his mother. Each time, I reject his request. Eventually, after years of the same dream, he stopped asking and simply played with me, enjoying our time together. Eventually, the dream ceased.

One day, I woke up to go to work, I opened my eyes, and I saw the little boy standing next to my bed. I said to him, "You again." Then, in a split second, I realized that I was awake. My eyes were wide open, and I was in my bedroom. I was not dreaming. Immediately, I got scared! At that instant, the image disappeared. I did not see him again! I guess that the little boy gave up on me and found a mother.

The reader can believe it or not. True or not true? It is true to me. Maybe other people had a similar experience. The story shows how our choices influence not only our own lives but also the lives of others. Free will is a profound gift that allows us to design our destiny, regardless of past circumstances.

Free will is a tool with no limitations to our spiritual self-evolution. We have the liberty to choose from the moment we wake up to our last breath of life. Our choices in life can determine what kind of life we want to live. Free Will is our action plan. We pick events that will help us to grow on a spiritual level. What we DO NOT choose is our reaction to those events. Our reactions are our life's lesson. *These reactions and actions create karma.*

It is fine if, at this moment in your life, you are skeptical about all these concepts. There is no urgency. You may not be ready yet for your next step. You will believe the above concept in due time, or *when you are ready to move forward in your own spiritual evolution.* Time is eternal. There is no rush!

Key Message: We are responsible for our actions. No one else can make those choices for us.

2. The Principle of Cause and Effect

This principle asserts that every action has an equal and opposite reaction. If we plant a maple seed, the result will be a maple tree, not an oak. Similarly, negative thoughts and emotions lead to adversity, while positive actions bring positive results.

Consider the profound impact of negative actions: Imagine if a person kills another person because of jealousy, or any personal reason, or for a radical belief, gang-related, etc. When we harm others, the repercussions extend far beyond the immediate act. In my interpretation, acts of violence or hatred create the most devastating karmic effects. Yet, for every positive deed, karma ensures that we are rewarded; perhaps not immediately, but in the future. If you do not experience the rewards of your kindness or good deeds in this lifetime, rest assured that they will manifest in the next.

A cause can have not one but multiple reactions. It is like a domino effect. Because of this principle, there is no such thing as "sin." God does not punish us for what we do. Religion does.

Society may punish us for a violation of its laws. However, an individual punishes or rewards themselves by what they *Think, Talk and Do*. The moment that a thought is created, it is already written in your book of life. Think consciously before you talk. Think consciously before you take any action. *Think of the consequences, and then choose.*

The principle of cause and effect is a fair principle. One cannot commit a crime and get away with it. The delinquent may escape from society but not from his or her own karma. The lawbreaker is trapped by his own criminal actions. The crime is written in his or her book of life.

Key Message: Cosmic justice always prevails. We may escape societal laws, but we cannot escape the law of karma.

3. <u>The Principle of Karma</u>

Karma is related to the principle of cause and effect. It dictates that we receive the consequences of our choices. The life you experience today is the result of the decisions and actions you have taken in the past.

We cannot change the past, but we can influence our future by applying the four principles I have outlined. The key is understanding that we are the architects of our own lives, and by embracing responsibility, we reclaim control.

Positive Karma can be cultivated by:

1) Analyzing your present circumstances, personally and professionally.

2) Examining your beliefs and thoughts, which will guide your transformation.

3) Neutralizing negative thoughts by not entertaining the same thoughts repeatedly. Replace them with positive ones.

4) Consciously repeat positive thoughts until they become ingrained habits.

5) Practicing patience and self-discipline as you forge a new path.

Read essay #3, "Snapshot of the Mind," to learn more tips on how to get rid of negative emotions.

Key Message: The problem of evil, sin, and wrongdoing resides in our beliefs, in our moral values, in our upbringing, in our organized society, and in our religious and political institutions.

4. The Principle of Repetition - Habits

Let us see how habits work.

The process of habit formation is the same, whether we are cultivating positive or negative habits. The difference lies in the outcome. To change, we must start with a *Strong Desire* to do things differently. Then, we must exercise *Patience*. Next, through *Self-Discipline,* we maintain focus, and finally, through *Action,* we embody the change we seek.

1. *Strong Desire to Change*

One must have a strong desire to do something different, such as to start a new career, business, or get rid of negative thoughts or behavior. The word desire is the key that will start the engine of the new "You."

2. *Patience:* A Reflection of Your Thoughts and Feelings

1) If you lose your patience, you will get angry and frustrated. Eventually, you will quit.

2) Getting angry is unhealthy; your blood pressure will go up, and your negative thoughts will be reinforced by the angry feeling.

3) Before you start the exercise, check your patience level by thinking about your expectations and any obstacles.

3. *Self-Discipline:*

41

1) Make a conscious choice to change negative thoughts into positive ones.

2) Decide to have patience and to go through this exercise.

3) Self-discipline will give you the strength to not quit.

4) Believe that you can overcome any barriers that come your way. Now, you know how to handle it.

5) You are in control of your thoughts and emotions all the time.

4. Action:

If you practice and practice, have patience with yourself, and have self-discipline, you will succeed. You already did steps two and three. "Action" is the continuation of both steps. Repeat Step #2 and #3 until you accomplish your goal.

When you catch yourself thinking or feeling negative, immediately STOP and change the thought into a positive one. You must do this switching as soon as the negative thought appears.

Remember:

1) It will take time.

2) Work on one thought at a time.

3) By switching the thought, you are creating a *new habit.* Make believe that your mind is a TV, and if you do not like what you see or hear, change the channel!

This process of converting negative thoughts into positive ones will help you create positive Karma. *Habits* are living creatures that are created in the subconscious mind over many years. We accumulate good and bad habits by us or by the influence of others (parents, family, or friends).

To unlearn, we need to know how the subconscious mind works. In essay 3 (Snapshot of the Mind), we will discuss how it works. In addition, see the 10 steps to get rid of bad habits. Appendix D

Key Message: By repeatedly choosing positive thoughts and actions, we create new habits. Habits that align with our Authentic Self.

Physical Self vs Spiritual Self

As we enter the 21ˢᵗ century, we find ourselves at the precipice of a new era. New technology has transformed our lives. This innovation is the effect of our energy-thought that we call "Intelligence" or, let us use our technology word, "Smart." Now, we have smartphones, smart TVs, smart watches, and so on.

However, it is important to remember that our true power lies not in gadgets or inventions, but in the potential of our minds. Imagine what would happen if we tapped into even a fraction of our mental capabilities.

Human beings go through different stages of life; infancy, childhood, adulthood, and maturity or third age. Scientifically, we understand this process. Physically, we are fully developed. Mentally, we are at the threshold of adulthood. This means that we have a long way to go. Part of the mental system is our feelings, emotions, and thoughts; each part is connected to the other as one mental unit.

Our intelligence permits us to recognize the physical self through our five senses; animals just try to survive through "animal instinct. Humans, not only survive but also preserve our experiences. What makes us human is our understanding of pain, happiness, love, life, and death.

The spiritual self is our invisible loving self. One cannot see it; however, it can be perceived through intuition and insights. It is the whispered voice within us.

Our body is a remarkable physical human machine, for the spiritual self to consciously grow. It must have a physical body!

The Spiritual Self needs its temporary companion life after life, until he or she completes the last cycle of spiritual evolution; at this stage, we are free. We no longer need the "Ego." The "I" of material possession. It is gone! The physical body is no longer needed. Free at last! The spiritual self is invisible, loving, and eternal. It is the part of us that whispers truth and guides us toward greater consciousness.

Key Message: To know your Authentic Self is to know your Divine Self. And once you know that, you will recognize that all of us are interconnected. We are part of a universal consciousness.

Reflection of Our Social and Political Self

We live in an age where technology offers incredible advancements, but it also makes us vulnerable to ignorant and dangerous minds. The dual nature of technology mirrors the duality of the self: it can be both a blessing and a curse.

Throughout history, humanity has suffered from ignorance and self-interest. These forces have fueled wars, atrocities, and injustice. Why the Inquisition? Why the holocaust? Why slavery? Why do wars still exist in the 21st century?

Possibly, because ignorance remains with us. *"Ignorance" is the virus of humanity, and Self-interest is its pestilence.* Unfortunately, some part of humanity still has a selfish mentality.

Why does war still exist? Who are the soldiers who go to war? And why do they go to war in the 21st century? I do not know the answer, but here is my interpretation. I see soldiers as our brothers and sisters, even our enemies. War should never be an option. Countries can negotiate their interest through diplomacy not war. Enough is enough!

Let us stop killing each other for more power and control.

No war justifies the loss of one human life, not even the life of the enemy. He or she is the son, the daughter, the husband, the wife, or the brother of another human being. War should never be an option!

It is painful to see cities destroyed by war, but more agonizing to lose thousands of human lives during war, and very distressing when there is no valid justification. Instead of war, we should have intelligent negotiations where the common denominator is a mutual interest between the countries involved.

The goal of any negotiation should be to benefit the country and its people. And when there is no agreement, *Compromise* is the next step. *War should never be an option.*

Unfortunately, corruption and self-interest are still alive in our society, still blooming in our institutions and governments around the world.

We must stop allowing greed and ignorance to govern our actions. Let us understand that life is unique and should not be wasted in wars. We must embrace love, justice, respect, compassion, and cooperation. These qualities are the foundation of our collective humanity.

Political Responsibilities

In any democracy, it is crucial that we understand our rights and responsibilities as citizens. In the United States, for example, while we may choose our local leaders through elections, the President is chosen by the Electoral College not by the popular vote.

The discrepancy calls for reform. Democracy is about the voice of the people. As a citizen, ask yourself this question: Shouldn't every vote count equally?

I hope that in my lifetime, there will be a reform in the election process. Instead of the Electoral College, we should accept the most votes as the final count. In this case, the majority is the "National Popular Vote." Our responsibility does not end with the vote. It continues in how we live and interact with the world.

Self-Responsibilities

Beyond our social and political obligations, we must also take responsibility for ourselves.. This involves:

1. Caring for our bodies through exercise and healthy eating.
2. Taking care of our minds by managing our thoughts and emotions.
3. Protecting our emotional well-being by eliminating stress and negativity.

These 3 elements are our own responsibility. If we do not take care of our own health and happiness, we become like a leaf moving around in the wind.

We must take charge of our lives; we must be the captain, the pilot, the driver of our lives.

The path to knowing your Authentic Self may not be easy, but it is worth the journey. The ancient Greek aphorism "Know Thyself" holds a timeless truth.

The reward of self-awareness is the discovery of your deepest truth… and that truth is divine.

BONUS

PROSE
OF
SELF

Perception of Self

Pendulum and evolution.
Ego, master of pleasures and desires.
Ring of colorful personalities.
Chamber of emotional struggles.
Erase all illusions of the mind.
Pre-conceived ideas must be erased.
Transform your thinking.
Intuition flows throughout your mind.
Original is its sound. You are the listener!
Never-ending voice of life is your intuition.

Overcome the personality.
Feel your body, sense your spirit.

Self-discovery is our journey.
Escape from the old, inflexible self.
Life is everywhere. Take a deep breath.
Feel and perceive your authentic self.

SEVEN PRINCIPLES OF LIFE

SPIRIT

Must be spirit before becoming physical.

ENERGY.

Must be energy before matter.

MIND.

It must be a thought before becoming a reality.

LIFE.

Must be born before dying.

GROWTH.

Must grow before perishing.

SOW.

Must sow before reaping.

KNOWLEDGE.

Must know before recognition.

SELF REDEFINED

Except human beings,
everything else comes with a manual.
Our parents did their best to figure it out,
how this little creature functions and lives.

Parents understand by instinct what the child needs.
Food, clothing, shelter, and most of all, love.
Can we blame our parents for our upbringing?
Can we blame ourselves if we become parents?

Human beings learn by trial and error.
One might ask the eternal questions.
Who Am I? What is life? What is death?
What is our purpose in life?

Philosophers, science, and religion,
tried to answer those questions.
It seems that there is no specific answer,
There are many ideas and concepts.

We get confused! Or we become skeptical.
Perhaps, we most consciously experience the self.
In each generation, there is constant change.
In each change, there is a part of the answer.

IT IS UP TO US

When we sleep.
We possess,
a galaxy of dreams,
and a world of nightmares.

When we are awake.
We possess,
a world of opportunities,
a universe of possibilities.

It is up to us!
To live.
Our dreams.
Or to live our nightmares.

It is up to us!
To re-direct our lives.
It is up to us!
To fulfill our self-discovery.

FIVE WAYS TO DEAL WITH DEATH

FIRST

Accept death as part of life.

SECOND

Read how other cultures deal with death.

THIRD

Review your own concept of death.

FOURTH

Prepare yourself for your own death.

FIFTH

Detach yourself from all material things.

LIFE MEASUREMENTS

How can a human being measure happiness?

By happiness.
By wealth.
By success.
By content.

How can a human being measure oneself?

By our own perception.
By the perception of others.
By what we do.
By what we say or think.

How can a human being measure love?

By Sexuality.
By Jealousy.
By Passion.
By Caring.

How can a human being measure life?

By breathing until it stops.
By Accomplishments or failures.
By Feelings and Reactions.
By Making mistakes and correcting them.

MISTAKES

The first mistake is a lack of knowledge.
The second mistake is ignorance.

To repeat the same mistake
over and over is foolishness.

Why does one make mistakes?
Two possibilities:

First, not enough information.
Second, too emotionally involved.

Whatever the case might be.
Do not feel sorry for yourself.

Do not make the same mistake.
Take responsibility for your actions.

Mistakes are part of life.
Learn the hidden lesson.

Accept, correct, and start again.
Never quit!

SELF-AWARENESS

Self-transformation is our aspiration.
Erase negativity, fear, and worries.
Love and respect yourself and others.
Follow your instinct, be silent, and listen!

Awareness of self is a process.
Where are you at this point in your life?
Are you happy? Are you worried?
Reflect, do not look back, and start again!
Elevate your consciousness.
Now is the time, to discover your authentic self.
Exclusive is the 21st century.
Self-awareness is its goal!

EVOLUTION

Evolutionary changes in nature.
Humanity absorbs those changes.

Physically.
We have reached the adulthood stage.

Mentally and emotionally.
We are at the threshold of adulthood.

Spiritually.
We are in the childhood stage.

It is time to know the authentic self.
It is time to recognize who we really are!

It is time to increase our mental capacity.
It is time to live our full potential.

PROCRASTINATION

In financial terms.
Procrastination equals poverty.

In job-related terms.
Procrastination equals deadline illusion.

In goal setting.
Procrastination equals germs.

In personal terms.
Procrastination equals no success.

In general.
Get rid of procrastination.

Before procrastination.
Infects your life and kills your dreams.

Get rid of procrastination.
Just do it now!

Desire is requisite.
Action is required!

ILLUSION OF SELF

My name and your name are not real.
Lilly, Benjamin, Jack, Blake, Sophia,
Leo, Aubrey, Autumn, Dylan,
Maxwell, Lorenzo, and Samuel are only names.
Fears, doubts, and worries are not real.
They are created by us! Our mind is the Creator.

We create our world according to our beliefs.
Look around you!
What do you perceive?
What are you constantly thinking about?
Are you satisfied with the way your life is?

If you do not like what you see.
Change your creation. We create harmony!
We create peace. We create wars.
We are the Creators!

It is insane to create distress and destruction.
When we can create peace and harmony.
Just by changing the way we think.
One can create peace and joy.
One can create love and happiness.

Do not believe in fear. It is an illusion!
Even your name is not real.
You and I have many names.
Recognize your real name.
And the illusion disappears.

"I AM,"
Is our real name
"I AM,"
is the authentic self.

THE PARK

Where am I?
I had a dream that I was the wind.

I had a dream that I was the rain.
I had a dream that I was the snow.

Clouds, witnesses of nature, where am I?
I cannot see myself, but I can see the sky.

I can see thousands of birds dancing in the sky.
I can see the storm getting closer to the park.

I can see the horizon and the ocean.
I can see children playing in the park.

I can see and feel, but no one can see me!
I know that I am alive.

I know that I existed before.
Trees, witnesses of nature, who am I?

The wind moves the dirt and papers.
Then a mysterious sound said:

Life is a swift moment!
You and all of us are just a few minutes of life.

Trees, witnesses of nature, where am I?
Wake up, darling!

Wake up! Wake Up!
You fell asleep in the park!

SIX INGREDIENTS OF LIFE

Change
Change is a requirement of life; it is not a choice.
Our option is to choose what will be the change.

Choice
When one decides…
One chooses its consequences.

Control
To consciously control our thoughts.
It is the key to stopping all the irregularities in our lives.

Happiness
If you put your happiness in other people's hands.
You will never be happy!

Time
Time is the most valuable commodity that we have.
Do not waste time! The clock is ticking!

Action
We must act or else ideas will crumble.
Action is the game of life.

THE RIDDLE OF SELF

Who am I?

The one that I perceive.
Or the one that people think I am?

I am what I dream, or I am what I feel.
I am what I think. Who am I?

Dreams are a fantasy of the night.
Nightmares are a chaos of the mind.

I dream of red clocks floating by the river.
Saying, "Time is running out."

I see an image of people dancing by the river.
What is the occasion? Asked the fisherman.

"There is no occasion," responded the eagle.
We all celebrate who we really are.

Is reality distorted by perception?
Or does perception create our reality?

Who am I?

DO IT TODAY

Today is the eternal present.
"I AM" is the present time

The past is gone; let it go!
Do not hold or live in the past.

Yesterday is gone!
"I WAS," is the past.

The future does not exist.
Do not live in the future.

The present is all yours.
Use the verb "I AM."

Get rid of "I was."
Get rid of "I will."

Use the present time.
I am living this moment!

Do it today! Do it now!
Tomorrow is the making of today!

NO ATTACHMENTS

Do not be attached to your body
You are not your body.

Just love it!
Just respect it!

Do not be attached to your race.
You do not belong to your country.

Just recognize it!
Just respect it!

Do not be attached to your religion.
Seek the true faith..

Seek, and seek! Do not quit!
You will find it!

Do not get caught between generations.
Do not live in the past or the future..

Live today. Live now!
The present is yours!

Do not be attached to physical positions
You are just a temporary owner.

Honor and respect life.
Life will respect you back!

SELF TRANSFORMATION

Stillness is the beginning of transformation.
Expansion of the mind is our cosmic connection.
Levels of consciousness live within us.
Fractions of truths begin to flow into our consciousness.

Thoughts become real. It is a principle!
Reality is perceived by our senses.
Awareness of self is our goal.
Nothing works until we recognize our authentic self.
Spirit is our reality. The spirit just IS!
Follow your intuition and open your mind.
Oneness is the unity of all. We are ALL ONE!
Rare breed of species. We think! We Act!
Marvelous brain. It is the temple of the mind.
Awareness of the real self is our next self-evolution.
Transformation and insights are our quest.
Inevitable is the change. We must know ourselves.
Override the old concept of self.
Necessary is the change for our own redemption.

GET READY

The zodiac sign of Aquarius is here!
The 20th century is gone! Let it go!
The 21st century is here!
Get ready!

Change and opportunities are its theme.
Get ready for choices and insights.
The time has come for self-awareness.
Get ready!

The Water Bearer is bringing inventions.
Truth, intelligence, and human kindness.
Change and transformation are in the air!
A constellation of prophecy is revealed!

A calendar of the cosmos is unfolding.
Page by page, year after year!
We must understand each symbol.
The 21st century is here! Get ready!

Be aware, be alert, and listen.
Listen to your inner voice.
The sign of Aquarius is whispering...
Get Ready! I AM here!

Remember Who You Are

Real or not real, truth or fiction.

Enchanted memories of life and dreams.

Memories of the past, fantasies of the future.

Entanglement moments in the present time.

Melodramas of expectations, past and present.

Belong or not to belong is the identity question.

Emotions, thoughts, illusions: a web of the mind.

River of experiences, pain, and passion intertwined.

Who am I? What do I think? What do I feel?

Holistic self or physical being, perhaps both.

Or simply: I AM.

You and I are universal beings.

One self, one spirit, many lives, many lessons.

Unlimited opportunities to know ourselves.

Awareness of the self is the key to remembering.

Reflect on your present life, recall your name.

Echo of self-resounding who you are.

ESSAY   #3

Snapshot of the Mind

An Interpretation of the Potential of the Mind

Thoughts arrive without invitation. If that is so, recognize the intruders—and one by one, transform them into "Control Thoughts," meaning: by invitation only.

What is the Mind?

In this essay, we explore three key manifestations of the mind, emphasizing that the mind is not merely a physical part of the brain. The three aspects we will delve into are:

1) The Conscious Mind, 2) The Subconscious Mind, and 3) The Super-Conscious Mind. To fully understand these elements, it is essential to consider the relationship between the mind and its physical counterpart, the brain.

However, before diving into the specifics of the mind's functions, let us touch upon other interpretations of the mind-body connection. Sigmund Freud, in his 1923 theory, identified the psyche as consisting of three parts: the id, the ego, and the superego. In psychology, the mind is often linked to awareness, cognition, consciousness, and emotion. In this essay, we combine the mind and body into a single entity, as they are deeply interconnected. Your mind and body are not separate; each influences the other. This symbiotic relationship can either enhance our well-being or deteriorate it.

While these two interpretations offer valuable insights, there are many others you might explore on your own. Ultimately, the question remains: who is in control? In my view, the mind is the boss. The brain should follow its commands.

This essay will focus on the human brain and its electrical activity.

We will examine how brain waves, measured by the electroencephalogram (EEG), operate across five distinct oscillation cycles. Understanding these cycles will provide insight into how we can use this information consciously, particularly during goal-setting and meditation. Mastery of this knowledge is the first step to taking charge of the mind.

The Electrical Activity of the Brain

Brain waves are categorized by their frequency, measured in cycles per second, or Hertz (Hz). The five primary oscillation cycles of the brain are:

Gamma rhythm: 30 to 100 Hz. This high-frequency wave occurs during intense concentration and learning.

Beta rhythm: 13 to 30 Hz. This is the state of heightened alertness, where we engage in problem-solving and decision-making.

Alpha rhythm: 8 to 12 Hz. Characterized by relaxation, this rhythm is associated with calm and mind-body communication.

Theta rhythm: 4 to 7 Hz. Often called the auto-pilot state, this rhythm occurs during deep relaxation, daydreaming, and meditation.

Delta rhythm: 1 to 4 Hz. The lowest frequency, linked to deep sleep and healing, though it can also indicate a flat EEG at less than 0.5 Hz, signifying cessation of brain activity.

Understanding these rhythms is crucial because they reveal how our mind and brain interact. We often operate on autopilot, unaware of the power we hold to direct our thoughts and behavior. By consciously engaging with these rhythms, we can gain control over the mind rather than letting the brain dictate our actions. By learning these 5 brain wave cycles, we can expand our attention, have less stress, and most of all, increase our control of the mind-brain.

Conscious Control of the Mind

The key question is: Who is the boss? In my view, the mind is the boss, and the brain is its tool. The brain is the physical manifestation of the mind, just as the body is the manifestation of the spirit.

The mind is the Commander in Chief; the brain must follow its orders. However, to become the master of the brain, we must first understand how the brain operates and how we can direct its activity.

To effectively direct the brain, we must reach the Alpha state, where we can access the Subconscious Mind and begin consciously directing our thoughts, beliefs, and goals. Here is how each of the five brain wave cycles relates to the mind, excluding Delta rhythm.

1) *Gamma* and *Beta* rhythms correspond to the *Conscious Mind,* where we process external information through our five senses. We are awake and alert.

2) *Alpha* rhythm corresponds to the *Subconscious Mind,* where relaxation, visualization, and meditation occur.

3) *Theta* rhythm is a blend of the Beta and Alpha rhythms, representing the *Superconscious Mind,* a state in which we can send directed thoughts to the Subconscious Mind, initiating a powerful shift toward self-mastery.

The Three Aspects of the Mind

The Conscious/Subconscious Mind :

The Conscious Mind is rational, analytical, and operates through our five senses. It is awake and engaged in daily life. In contrast, the *Subconscious Mind* is subjective, emotional, and creative. It works 24/7, recording everything we experience, even while we sleep. Imagine if this recording becomes real, we probably would develop another branch of psychiatry.

The Subconscious Mind needs to hear the same idea or affirmation repeatedly until it gets the visual message or affirmation. The name of the game is repetition. This is how we create habits by repeating the same behavior until it becomes automatic in us. The subconscious mind is "blind" in the sense that it accepts everything without question.

For instance, if someone tells you that a pen is blue, and you close your eyes and trust the information, the Subconscious Mind accepts it as truth, until you open your eyes and see otherwise.

The Subconscious Mind, though blind, is a powerful tool when used consciously, especially for practices like visualization. In this level, we can create new habits or innovative ideas.

The Superconscious Mind transcends both the Conscious and Subconscious Minds. It is our hidden treasure, a space of infinite potential where we connect with our Authentic Self and the Cosmic Consciousness. To access this state, we must consciously direct our thoughts and beliefs, creating a bridge between the conscious and the subconscious. This is where true mastery of the mind begins.

Reaching the Superconscious Mind

To access *the Superconscious Mind*, we must cultivate conscious **awareness** and direct the Subconscious Mind with purpose. This can be done through meditation, focused visualization, and intentional goal-setting. In this state, we connect not only with our higher selves but also with the *Cosmic Consciousness.* The source of all wisdom and creation. If we do this while we are in the alpha cycle, we can accomplish any goal that we set for ourselves. The Cosmic Consciousness will be discussed in the next essay.

When one reaches a "conscious" communication between the mind and the brain, the effect is total awareness of body, mind, and spirit. We are no longer reacting to life's events like puppets.

The **Subconscious Mind** functions through three primary channels.

- 1. **The Thought Channel:** *What We Think.*
- 2. **The Words Channel:** *What We Say.*
- 3. **The Visualization Channel:** *What We See and imagine in our mind*

Each of these channels influences our emotions and behavior. When we direct our thoughts, words, and use visualization consciously and repetitively, we program the Subconscious Mind for success. Each channel increases by feelings and by repetition.

In addition, *we must be aware of our daily thinking.* We must close the road of negative thinking and create a new road of positive thinking. Let us not waste more time.

In this essay, I just want to give you a taste of your own potential. The first thing that you need is the desire to change. Second, you need to *convey the same idea (goals) to the subconscious mind in a conscious way.* Repeatedly. Repeat and repeat with conviction.

In the short term, you can use any goal, such as to be successful in your profession, to lose weight, to quit smoking, to start a new business, etc. You will design your life the way you want it to be.

Create a new profile of yourself. But keep in mind *the must-do list:*

1) Consciously direct your thoughts.

2) Consciously visualize your goal.

3) Consciously prepare a list of affirmations. (See Appendix A for affirmations.)

4) Consciously get rid of negative thoughts.

5) Consciously believe in your goal and persist until you get it.

6) Consciously concentrate and focus on your goal.

If you do not get your goal by doing the above list, it means: First, that there is too much noise in your subconscious mind; therefore, you need to begin to relax and meditate. (See appendix B for breathing and relaxation exercises.) Second, you need to get rid of negative thoughts before you begin with any goal.

(See essay 2. The Principles of Repetition-Habits.)

Mastering the Channels

1. THOUGHT CHANNEL: *What We Think.*

Our thoughts shape our reality. If you entertain negative thoughts, such as fear, anger, worry, etc., these become habits. The goal is to recognize these negative patterns and consciously replace them with positive thoughts.

Here are the eight most negative thoughts or emotions that we should get rid of one by one. If you do not have or entertain any of those negative thoughts, Bravo for you!

1. Anger
2. Fear
3. Hate
4. Worry
5. Doubt
6. Envy
7. Greed
8. Resentment

The problem with these eight thoughts-feelings is when they become habits, due to their repetition of the same thought or emotion day after day, year after year. These habits stick with you, marking your personality, and eventually they come to invade your life like a virus.

Let us pause for a second and go over the eight negative feelings. If you believe that you entertain any of those negative emotions, begin the process of elimination.

We should get rid of any bad emotions before those feelings consume our physical body and contaminate our mind.

The key to getting rid of a negative thought is by:

1) Taking conscious control of your thinking.

2) Deciding *consciously* to eliminate them.

3) Creating a new thought consciously.

Remember, you must always substitute a negative thought for a positive one. By doing these 3 steps, you create a new path.

In addition, as soon as you wake up, say the following affirmations to yourself.

"Today, I Erase "Anger" from my vocabulary.

"Today, I erase 'Fear' from my vocabulary.

Today, I erase 'Worries" from my mind

"Today, I am Happy."

"Today, I Am Calm and Feel Peaceful."

"Today, I Have Confidence in Myself"

"Today, I Can Do It!"

Say those affirmations or create your own according to your needs. You are the Creator!. Repeat the same affirmations every day until they become part of you.

It is extremely important to become aware of these eight negative emotions; so, every time that you feel one of them, you *consciously* acknowledge it and immediately correct it. This is called self-awareness.

Just by consciously correcting the wrong thought or feeling, you will expand your consciousness. This switch of thoughts will create a new habit in your life. It will bring you to a higher level of consciousness. No one can do it for you. Only YOU can shape your life; within us lies the raw material of spiritual life. Try to keep in your mind only goodness, kindness, compassion, and love for yourself and others.

We, as mortal individuals, tend to contaminate our lives with our thoughts and actions. We are ignorant of the power of our mind; it is not our fault. We are ignorant of our authentic self, the Spiritual Self, the eternal Self. Fortunately, life forgives our mistakes repeatedly. Time never rushes. *Our Spiritual Self is patiently waiting for our awakening!*

2. WORDS CHANNEL: What We Say.

Words are a direct link to the Subconscious Mind. When we say "I am weak" or "I am unhappy," we send a message to our brain to manifest those feelings. Conversely, affirming "I am strong." Confident," or "I am at peace," shifts our state of being.

Why? Because if someone says: I am weak, I am depressed, the subconscious-mind is listening and, if you keep saying the same words over and over, the sub-conscious-mind says: Ok, let me send the message to your brain-body so you can begin to feel what you are asking for in a form of stress, headache, anxiety, etc.

If you say the opposite, I am happy, I feel lucky today, I am blessed, and even if you do not have the feeling yet, make believe that you are an actor and play the role.

The subconscious mind then says, "I am listening," and suddenly you feel happy and opportunities arrive. Why? Because what we are doing is dictating to the subconscious mind what we want to feel and think. Next, the conscious mind receives the message and immediately sends it by express mail to the mind-brain. The mind obeys your Conscious Orders, and your messages become real.

Try to follow the exercise below; it can help you become aware of your self-talk. Begin now to *Catch Yourself* every time you mention either "I" or "I AM."

1) Write the phrase on a piece of paper.

2) Do not analyze it yet.

3) Do this for 3 consecutive days.

4) Then make a list of the positive and negative statements associated with "I" or "I AM."

This exercise will make you conscious of what you say all day long. Remember that what you say relates to what you think, feel, and believe. Our words are the expression of our thoughts and feelings.

The first thing that one must do is to change not the feeling, *but the thinking*. Feelings are just symptoms. It is our reaction to something outside or inside us that makes us feel negative or positive. *What We Think is the Cause, Not the Effect. The effect is on our emotions.*

From your "I AM" list, enhance all the positive affirmations and examine all the negative ones. Both expressions characterize what you think. Therefore, it represents the *essence of you*. Negative statements must be eliminated from your mind, vocabulary, and from your heart (your feelings). One way to correct them is by using the opposite word (antonyms). By doing this, all the negative feelings will disappear one by one. It is also good to write on an index card the following reminder. Post it in a place where you can see it every day. Remember, repetition is the key to success.

Be patient with yourself!

> *Do Not Procrastinate*
> *Do Not Quit!, Do Not Quit!*
> *Decide now what you want!*
> *You are the Creator!*

3. **VISUALIZATION CHANNEL:** *What we see and imagine in our mind.*

Visualization is the act of mentally rehearsing our goals. By focusing on a vivid image of our desired outcome, we create a blueprint in the mind that guides our actions toward fulfillment.

These images are created on our mental screen. Our imagination will paint a picture. Our enthusiasm will make the feeling come alive. When we have all the above ingredients in place, we begin the visualization process on our mental screen.

We just focus our attention on this visualization. If, for any reason, we notice something that we do not like. We can change it and keep visualizing. The key here is not to entertain yourself with thoughts other than your goal. Concentration is vital for success.

However, most of the time we function in an automatic mode. Thoughts come uninvited. It can be negative thoughts, such as worries and fears, etc., or positive. If you want to take control of your thinking, start working on the following:

1.   *We Must Change Our Way of Thinking.*

2.   *We Must Give the Mind a Definite Order!*

3.   *We Must Take Conscious Control of our Thoughts.*

4.   *We Must Disconnect Ourselves from the Automatic Self.*

5.   *We Must Stop Our Mind from Thinking in a Disorganized Way.*

6.   *Remember, "You are the boss!*

In addition to having your complete attention on your goal. You must do the following:

1) Consciously, believe in yourself.

2) Consciously, prepare your goal.

3) Consciously, create your own affirmations.

4) Reinforce your goal with affirmations and meditation

5) Focus, concentrate, and pay attention to your goal.

6) DO NOT QUIT! And DO NOT QUIT!

To visualize your goal is your responsibility. Your subconscious mind will do its part. The outcome cannot be other than VICTORY!

Now ask yourself this question: How Much Time Do I Spend in Using My Mind in a Conscious and Directed Way? We know the answer: "Not much time." Why is it that we do not spend enough time learning how to use our mind-brain?

These are some speculations to think about:

> a) We do not know the connection between our Finite mind and our Infinite Mind.
>
> b) We do not know our connection between our mind and the Cosmic Mind
>
> c) We do not know our own potential or personal power.
>
> d) We do not know the power of our thoughts.
>
> e) We do not know that life is a thought.

The reader can add their own speculation. Just remember that you have the potential to be what you want! But, conscious action is required!

Be the Creator of your Life! It is your Birth Right!

Good Luck!

Essay Summary

Our brain is a complex organ; my intention is to focus on the electrical activity of the brain. The Electroencephalogram, or the EEG, measures our brain waves. There are 5 oscillation cycles:

Gamma rhythm (good concentration). Beta rhythm (we are alert). Alpha rhythm (relaxed mind, and body communication). Theta rhythm (day dreaming). Delta rhythm (deeply sleeping, healing begins).

To reach the Alpha level is the key to connect with our subconscious mind as well as to get rid of negative thoughts such as hate, fear, doubt, etc. The idea is to consciously direct our goals and desires during this relaxed state. It is crucial to learn how to relax and to lower our brain activity. At the Alpha level, we are in direct contact with our subconscious, super-conscious mind, and our authentic self, which is our spiritual self. In addition, we are in contact with the Cosmic Consciousness or Infinite Intelligence.

There are three aspects of the mind. First, the Conscious-Mind, which is the rational, logical mind. Our 5 senses are alert. Second, the subconscious mind, which is ruled by our habits and our belief system. The subconscious mind works day and night. Third, the Super-Conscious Mind, at this state, we are aware of our authentic self and our connection with the Cosmic Consciousness.

These three manifestations of the mind communicate with each other through three channels. 1) the Thought channel (what we think), 2) the Words channel (what we say), and 3) the Visualization channel (what we see and imagine in our mind).

The Power of Repetition

Repetition is the key to programming the Subconscious Mind. Positive affirmations, visualizations, and thoughts, when repeated consistently, reshape our reality. The more we practice these techniques, the more ingrained they become in our minds and behaviors.

If you struggle to achieve your goals, it may be due to negative subconscious programming or mental clutter. Relaxation techniques and meditation can help clear the mental noise, allowing you to align your subconscious with your conscious desires.

Conclusion: You Are the Creator of Your Life

The mind is a powerful tool, but too often we let it control us. By understanding the electrical activity of the brain and how our thoughts, words, and visualizations influence our behavior, we can take conscious control of our lives.

Remember, you are the creator of your life. Our thoughts shape your reality by mastering the three aspects of the mind. Conscious, Subconscious, and Superconscious, you can unlock your true potential and achieve anything you set your mind to.

Take Conscious Action. You Are the Creator.
Your future awaits!

BONUS

PROSE
OF THE
MIND

CREATION

In one poem exists a rhyme.
In one life exists a thought.
In one thought exists a universe.

Reflect, meditate, and listen.
We are the thought of the Creator.
We are the rhyme and the music.

Create your life with your mind.
You are the artist!
If we control our thoughts,
We become masters of our lives.

Change your negative thoughts.
To positive actions.
Become aware of what you think.

The rhythm of life is within you.
Listen to its music and dance.
Meditate and review your thoughts.

Transform your old thinking.
Contemplate your life and listen.
Listen to the thought of creation!

STOP NEGATIVE THINKING

Learn to be motionless.
Learn to be silent.
Relax and calm your senses!
Stop Random Thinking!

Listen to your inner voice.
Meet your real self.
Awake from the illusion.
Of living in constant crisis.

Free yourself from fear.
Do not embrace pain.
Do not accept misery.
Move away from reactions.

Get rid of your conditional self.
Free yourself from your old creation.
Create a conscious self.
Create a new "You."

Welcome the flow of life.
Let life reveal your identity.
Listen to your secret name.
Perceive its meaning.

Learn to be still.
Learn to be soundless.
Listen to your heartbeat.
It is the sound of life.

GOOD LUCK CHARMS

If you wear it or carry it.
If it is a crystal or a stone.
It does not matter.

The object does not contain "the luck."
Luck is your belief.
The object does not matter!

Nothing moves or works at random.
The conscious mind moves everything.
Your thoughts do matter!

Luck!
Is a wave of possibility!
Faith is an ocean of security!

Believe!
Is the luck that matters!
Believing is your lucky charm!

THE POWER OF CHOICE

Negative and Positive thoughts.
Both have the same power.

Negative and positive emotions.
Both have the same power.

Our choice predicts the consequences.
It is not the circumstance. It is not luck!

It is not fate! It is our choice!
Our decision makes it better or worse.

If we choose Red Roses.
Red Roses we get!

If we plant apples or grapes.
Apples and grapes we get!

It is the principle of Cause and Effect.
Free Will is our heritage.

Our future depends on our choices.
What you choose today is your future!

WAKE ME UP FAIRY OF THE NIGHT

Poetry is the night!
Mystery and Legends!

A dream is a poem.
Image is a verse.

Hallucination of the senses!
Conflict of the ego!

Endless minutes in the dark.
The brain is drowsy!

Visions and tormented sounds.
Wake me up, Fairy of the Night!

I see six Fairies holding a string of light!
Behind them, a constellation of stars!

Is this a dream?
Wake me up! Wake me up!

Is this a game of the mind?
Puzzle of memories and fantasy!

Reality misread by perception.
Legends of fairies and monsters.

Wake me up! Wake me up!
Fairy of the Night!

THE JOY OF LIVING

Reject all negative thinking.
Repel lust and greed.

Drive away from anger and rage.
Jealousy, resentment, and envy.

These are illnesses of the soul.
These are corruptions of the body.

Instead, spread enthusiasm.
Reach out to others with respect.

Explore your options.
Search for possibilities.

Find the joy of living.
One day at a time!

CHANGE YOUR THINKING

Eliminate negative thoughts of the past.
Eliminate negative thoughts of the present.
Eliminate all your negative thoughts.
Change your thinking!

To change negative thoughts.
Action is required! Desire is a must!
To redirect your thinking is your goal.
Not to quit is your success!

Keep only positive thoughts in your mind.
Your mind obeys your desires. Be the captain!
Be aware of what you think and feel..
If it is negative, change your Thinking!

It is your choice. Choose to be happy!
Smile and dance, smell the roses, feel the air.
Change your thinking! It will change your life.
Think positively. You are the artist of your life.

TODAY I CHOOSE

Today
I am conscious of myself.

Today
I choose to have a positive attitude.

Today
I will not criticize or judge.

Today
I get rid of negative thoughts.

Today
I stop my thoughts from running wild.

Today
I am responsible for my thoughts.

Today
I am responsible for my choices.

Today
I create my life with my thoughts.

Today
I choose to respect and tolerate others.

Tomorrow
I choose what I am choosing today.

DO NOT WORRY

About problems.
Each problem,
contains its own solution.

In each solution
There are options

In each change,
Resides a challenge.

In each challenge,
There is personal growth.

It takes time.
To learn not to worry.

It takes time.
To control your thoughts.

Transform your thinking.
"Worry" is just a word.

THE DREAMER

The dreamer sleeps in a huge, puffy cloud.
Unicorns and fairies pass by,
fantasy mixed with reality.
The night is full of images and nightmares.
The wind dances in a perfect path.
The muse carries the dreamer.

2

The day is filled with expectations.
Daydreaming is our magic shield.
Is the dreamer awake or asleep?
Perception paints our senses.

3

The wind dances around the cloud.
The motion creates a sound.
The echo awakens the dreamer.
The dreamer is awake!
The wind gently, softly whispers.
Go back to sleep. Go back!
I will teach you the sound of creation!

NEGATIVE EMOTIONS

Anger is a negative emotion.
New and old resentment.
Gap of love and goodwill.
Emotion uncontrolled.
Re-establish control.

And harmony will reign!

Hate is a disturbing emotion.
Aversion to people and things.
Turbulence of the heart.
Equilibrium must be established.

And harmony will reign!

Rage fury of the soul.
Action out of control.
Gate of destruction.
Establish conscious control.

And harmony will reign!

FREE ASSOCIATION

A poet creates a verse.
A painter creates a portrait.
Since I am not a poet.
I paint a poem of love.

Strange poem!

The one who paints is not a painter.
The one who writes is not a poet.
Ideas, words, and thoughts.
Music, poetry, and colors.
Ensemble of sounds and vibrations.

Rainbow of lights and creation!

Perfect design of the universe.
Art supreme expression of the mind.
Majestic is the form of nature.
Life is captured in an instant.
Death is embraced by the soul.
Humanity is a flick of reality!

Divine is the imagination!

CYCLES OF LIFE

Rain, Summer, Fall, Winter.
Seasons, cycles of nature.
Thoughts, visions of the mind.

Life
Is a constant change.

Living
Is a daily choice.

Be aware of your decision.
Be responsible for its consequences.

Self-evolution.
Is the goal of oneself!

Thoughts
Image of the consciousness-mind.

Perception
Illusion of the senses!

Life is not an accident.
To live or not to live.
Is our choice!

BETWEEN YOU AND ME

Between now and then, there is a story.
Between the sky and the earth, there is space.
Between the ocean and the sand, there is the wave.
Between goals and dreams, there is work.
Between black and white, there is gray.
Between you and success, there is a space.
Between you and time, there is a season.
Between the seasons, there is life.
Between life and death, there is a moment.

Discover yourself. Find the space.
Find the season. Live the moment.
Do not waste more time. Do it now.
Between words and thoughts, there is the world.
Between you and yourself, there is another.
Between the brain and the mind, there is the imagination.

IS YOUR CHOICE

Life is a risky choice.
When one takes a risk.
One wins or loses.
No risk means total loss!

To love or not to love.
To work or not to work.
To risk or not to risk.
What would you choose?

To live is a choice.
To work is a choice.
To study is a choice.
Life is a constant choice!

Whatever you choose, you get!
Whatever you think, you get!
What would you choose?
To choose is up to you!

CHANGE, TRANSFORM AND REPEAT

Substitute Anger with goodwill.

Swap Worry Thoughts for positive ones.

Trade Resentment for forgiveness.

Change Fear to acting calm. Be an actor!

Switch Doubt to confidence.

Exchange Greed for generosity.

Transfer Envy to kindness.

Replace Hate with Love.

ESSAY   #4

Snapshot of God and the Universe

An Interpretation with a Touch of Imagination

What is life? Life is a state of consciousness. If that is so, who am I? You, too, are a state of consciousness. If that is so, what is my purpose? To consciously know what you are, perhaps, you are a thought in the mind of God.

Is the Universe God's Creation or a Big Bang moment!

Who Is God For You?

Throughout history, every culture has personalized God, shaping God into a form that fits their society's needs. Sometimes to serve political or material purposes, and at other times to address spiritual needs. Culture, religion, and society all play significant roles in how we understand God. However, despite these influences, our higher Self knows the truth. It is this Higher Self that recognizes that God's nature is universal, transcending labels and images shaped by human hands.

To truly understand this concept, we must release the "customized labels" created by culture, religion, and society about God, as well as the humanized image we have imposed on God. From my perspective, God does not belong to a specific culture, tribe, group, or race. God is Universal. God is the One Source of Life, the One Cosmic Consciousness, the One Intelligence, the One Infinite Love. It is through this Spirit of Love and the Mind of God that we energize our mind and heart alike.

We, the children of God, are connected to God through our Higher Self. By tapping into this Infinite Mind, we begin to recognize that we are one with the Universal God, united with the Oneness of God.. This shared connection makes us brothers and sisters, an inseparable unity of the Human Spirit.

Because defining God is inherently challenging, I prefer the term "perception" over "definition." Let us explore three fundamental questions, and through these questions, allow you, the reader, to form your own interpretation of God.

Question 1: Is the Universe God's Creation, or is it a Big Bang Moment?

Question 2: Did Space and Time Exist Before the Big Bang?

Question 3: If So, How Was Space Created Before and After the Big Bang?

Exploring the Big Bang and God's Role:

Current scientific understanding, as of 2025, tells us that the universe began 13.8 billion years ago with the Big Bang, a massive, turbulent explosion. From this moment, all matter, as we know it, emerged. Some astronomers suggested the universe will continue expanding forever, while others predict it will eventually freeze or collapse. But the question remains: can we, fragile mortals, deny the existence of God?

We may not have the ability to physically observe beyond our current scientific knowledge, but if we use intuition and imagination, we may gain deeper insights into the universe's creation and our connection to God. Through the lenses of intuition, imagination, and insight, we can approach the mystery of God's presence in our universe.

Question #1: The Universe: God's Creation or a Big Bang Moment?

To answer both parts of this question, I say, "Yes." The first part, "Is the universe God's creation?" belongs to the Infinite Concept. This concept has no beginning or end. It is self-existing, self-creative, eternal, and endless. Essentially, it is God's Consciousness. The Infinite Concept is the non-physical foundation of everything.

The second part, "Is creation the Big Bang?" belongs to the Finite Concept. The Finite Concept represents the physical materialization of the Infinite Concept. It is the world of energy and matter that we experience in our 3rd dimension. The physical world is temporarily and constantly in transformation. The Big Bang marked the beginning of our physical universe, and though it had a beginning, it is part of a larger, endless process of transformation. Death, in the cosmic sense, does not exist; only life and creation continue to evolve. Its first name is Duplication, its middle name is Repetition, and its last name is Transformation.

Formula: Duplication +Repetition=Transformation

The universe is full of life. Our physical universe is a vibration of matter and energy, where energy converts into matter, and matter converts back into energy. This mirrors Einstein's equation $E=mc^2$. Each concept (Infinite and Finite) has its own set of rules; nevertheless, they are not separate concepts. They are Two-Fold Concepts.

Through the lens of both ancient mythologies and modern scientific discoveries, here is my interpretation of the Big Bang and the creation of the cosmos. I base this on two theories and three principles.

Theory #1 Cosmic Memory and Dimensional Hierarchy. Theory #2 The Unity Theory and the Power of Numbers. Three Principles: 1) Cosmic Memory Universe, 2) The Opposite-Double 3) Duplication, Repetition and Transformation.

THEORY #1

COSMIC MEMORY AND DIMENSIONAL HIERARCHY

Inverted Pyramid - Dimensional Hierarchy

4 Invisible Minutes Before the Big Bang.

3 Visible Minutes the Big Bang, 2nd D, and 3rd D.

Figure.1

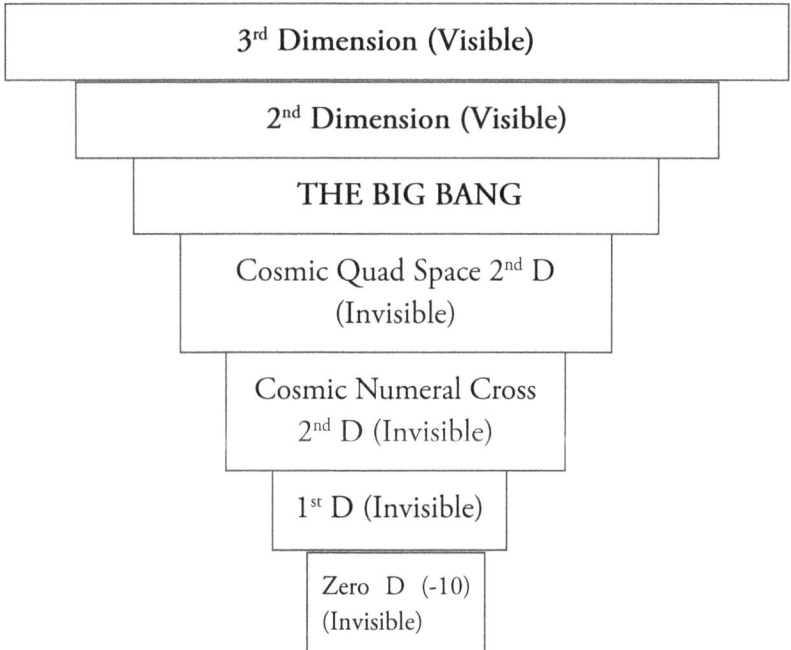

Theory #1:

Cosmic Memory and Dimensional Hierarchy

The cosmos, as I imagine it, is a Dimensional Hierarchy, represented by an inverted pyramid. (Figure.1) The concept suggested that everything that exists has "memory" of how it evolves and transforms from stars to galaxies, from cells to organisms.

Everything that exists remembers how to live, grow, develop, and transform itself into something else. This Cosmic Memory is part of God's Consciousness, embedded in energy waves throughout the cosmos.

The top of the inverted pyramid, which is the bottom or the apex, represents the highest level of energy (Zero Dimension). It represents the origin of all physical and non-physical existence. As the pyramid expands, dimensions form and evolve, creating a continuum of existence in both visible and invisible states.

In this hypothetical story, God created the cosmos with numbers, which is not a new idea. The concept of numbers goes back to ancient Greece. "Pythagoras believes that numbers are behind all things."

The structure of space in this theory is created with geometrical figures, as we will see in detail later in this essay. But for now, here is a sneak preview of the inverted pyramid. The apex stands for number minus ten (-10), (mathematics) or a point (geometry). The apex represents Zero Dimension, a position in space and the beginning of our physical universe.

The second level represents a horizontal line or the First Dimension. The third level represents the crossing of the horizontal and vertical lines at the center or (-10), the origin. This crossing creates a cross. I call it. The Cosmic Numeral Cross (CNC). When the Cosmic Numeral Cross repeats the motion up/down/left/right infinitely, it creates an invisible blueprint of the 2nd Dimension, which I named the CosmicQuad Space (CQS). Then *Boom, Boom, the Big Bang was born.*

The fifth level represents the 2nd visible dimension of space, which expands by the Power of 2. Each level builds on the one before it in a connected memory system. The sixth level is our 3rd dimension.

Three Principles

1. Cosmic Memory Universe

The first principle says: *All creation begins in the Universal Cosmic Mind* as memory, before any physical form.

This manifestation is the birth of physical matter, and the memory of this creation persists in the cosmos. Each newborn "matter" has a memory of its own self with the power to create, re-create, and transform itself into new forms. This process is encoded in the Dimensional Hierarchy. Perhaps we can imagine the cosmos as a huge invisible brain that belongs to God Consciousness, or if you prefer, the Universal Cosmic God.

2. The Opposite-Double

The second principle says: *Every Physical form has a Non-Physical Counterpart: its Memory-Energy-Double.* The *Memory-Energy Double*, sustains and transforms it. Keep in mind that every system, every principle, evolves from the previous one. Absolutely nothing can survive alone, even if you see it alone. In fact, everything that exists has an opposite double, just like a mirror image of itself; such as a physical body and spirit, matter, and anti-matter, etc.

3. Duplication, Repetition, and Transformation

The third principle says: *The Creative Driving Forces of the Universe are: Self-Duplication, Repetition, and Transformation.*

Each time a system duplicates and repeats, it evolves into something new, creating a cycle of transformation from atoms to molecules, from molecules to complex forms of life. This is the simplest of the three principles and the most creative. *First it duplicates, repeats, and then transforms.*

The cosmos is simple in its creation, but complex in its effects and transformation. It is a chain of memory systems and sub-systems. For example, in chemistry, the periodic table of chemical elements (a system) started with the first element, Hydrogen. Its atomic mass is the lightest of all elements. After hydrogen comes the next element, helium, and so on; each element increases its atomic mass. As of 2025, the last element discovered is #118 Oganesoon (Og). Even though element #119, as of now, is hypothetical (Ununennium), each element is part of the previous element. We humans are bio-chemical-electro bodies with 60% of water in our bodies (Hydrogen and Oxygen). Hydrogen is the mighty unity that unites all chemical elements, including us. Gravity is the King of energy force in the 3rd Dimension. In other dimensions, Gravity takes his crown off.

According to this interpretation, it is important to understand the two concepts (Infinite and Finite) as well as the two theories and the three principles, because they are the basis of everything that exists in the universe. To help you visualize the Two-In-One concept. See figure 2.

Chart: A to D   The Cosmos

Figure. 2

A	B	C	D
Invisible	Invisible	Finite Space	Visible
Cosmic Memory Universe	Infinite Space	Help of Telescopes	Physical world

Since our senses are very limited, as is our telescope, we are unable to see the total spectrum of the Cosmos, which is from A to D. *A* and *B* are invisible to our modern technology. *C,* we need the help of telescopes. *D* is our visible physical world. Unfortunately, our physical eyes and telescopes can only see a small portion of the spectrum of the cosmos.

However, the new James Webb telescope might surprise us with new discoveries.

Summary of Theory #1 and the 3 Principles

Question One: The Universe: God's Creation or a Big Bang Moment?

The answer is YES, God is the Creator, and it belongs to the Infinite Concept. The second part of the question is also YES. It belongs to the Finite Concept. The Big Bang marks the beginning of our physical world.

The Infinite and Finite Concepts are two aspects of one whole. God as Creator is ever-present across all dimensions, where each level builds on the one before. It is one concept with three basic, simple principles. I use the word "simple" because the language of GOD is *Simplicity*. God uses simplicity in all creations.

Theory #1 Cosmic Memory and a Dimensional Hierarchy.

This theory presents the universe as an inverted pyramid of dimensions, starting with Zero Dimension and culminating in the visible 3rd Dimension. The four invisible minutes before the Big Bang introduce: Zero and First Dimension. The Cosmic Numeral Cross and the Cosmic Quad Space. The Big Bang (minute 5) marks the shift into the finite world.

Summary of 3 Principles

Principle#1 Cosmic Memory Universe

All things begin as thought, conceived in the Universal Cosmic Mind before manifesting physically.

Principle#2 The Opposite-Double

Every physical form is paired with a non-physical counterpart, its memory-energy double.

Principle#3 Duplication, Repetition, and Transformation

The creative driving force of the universe repeats itself in cycles: everything duplicates, repeats, and transforms.

Question #2: Did Space and Time Exist before The Big Bang?

The answer is YES for space and NO for time. Time does not exist in the Infinite Concept. Time is the eternal "Now."

Time began with the birth of the physical universe, an illusion of the past, present, and future. Time is merely a measurement that emerged with the Finite Concept, while the Infinite Concept is beyond time and always present.

Question #3: How was space made before and after the Big Bang? (The answer is theory #2)

Theory #2: The Unity Theory and the Power of Numbers

Space, before and after the Big Bang, is rooted in the power of numbers. The Unity Theory states that everything in the universe is interconnected. Numbers and geometrical shapes create the structure of space.

Its abstract nature belongs to the Infinite Concept, while its physical nature (Mathematics) belongs to the Finite Concept. Here lies the first duality of the cosmos.

I would like to invite the reader to visualize this concept as well as to use their imagination during the first four invisible minutes *before* the Big Bang and the first three visible minutes *after* the Big Bang (7 minutes in total).

The first four minutes are part of the physical world, but it is invisible to us; so, let the imagination begin.

Once upon a time, there was a thought and two numbers. Number One (1) and Number Zero (0). Both were floating in an infinite space, after eons of time floating around, number One and number Zero saw each other for the first time. The attraction was so strong that in an instant, they fused together and became number minus ten (-10).

NOTE: (If zero (0) is negative, and number one (1) is positive, the result is negative; therefore, we have minus ten (-10).

At this critical moment, let us call number one (1) Gravity, and positive. Electricity, number zero (0) and negative. Both became the point in geometry or number minus ten (-10), the apex of the inverted pyramid. See Figure 1 (page 105).

Now the reader can envision the cosmos as a manifestation of God's thinking. God used *Numbers* to create the cosmos and *Geometrical shapes* to create the structure of space.

The reader probably heard the expression that God is a Geometer, an Architect, and a Mathematician. I am sure that the reader also heard the motto of Pythagoras that *Numbers are behind everything that exists.* In my humble opinion, I believe that Pythagoras was right not only with his concept of numbers but with his theorem of the right triangle. Pythagoras's equation $a^2 + b^2 = c^2$ is the basic micro-unit of our physical space. In this theory, Pythagoras's equation is the key that opens the door to the structure of space, as the reader will see later in this essay.

In this theory, the cosmos is built upon geometric and numerical foundations, shapes and structures emerge from the repetitive motion of energy and matter, from the first triangle to the complex forms of galaxies.

First Invisible Minute Before the Big Bang

Minute #1 The Creation of Zero Dimension

Let us visualize number minus ten (-10) as the origin emerging as a point in an infinite space. Let us remember when number one (1) Gravity (positive) met number zero (0) Electricity (negative), fell in love, and the union brought into being number minus ten (-10). In this theory, mathematics and geometry go hand in hand. *The point or number minus ten (-10) represents zero or NO Dimension and a Position in space.* The Number minus (-10) represents negative energy.

Number minus (-10) or the Point (.)

Figure. 3 **Zero Dimension**

In this theory, the number minus (-10) is the source of cosmic energy. It contains the memory of the encounter of number (1) and number zero (0) fusing together as number minus (-10).

Number minus (-10) holds the memory of everything and the beginning of everything.

Number minus ten (-10) is pure memory-energy and the unified Cosmic Force. It carries Gravity and Electricity, their union of love produced Electro-Magnetisms, Strong Nuclear force, and the Weak Nuclear force, as *one Cosmic Memory-Energy force.* These energy forces are the four fundamental forces that govern our universe today.

Note: Zero dimension represents the apex of the inverted pyramid.

Second Invisible Minute before the Big Bang

Minute #2 Invisible First Dimension

The point or number minus ten (-10) is going to spread out its arms negative from 10 to 1 in descending order, going "outward" on the right and left sides, and positive from 1 to 10 going "inward" on both sides. See Figure. 4

Left side (outward-negative) and inward-positive

01 02 03 04 05 06 07 08 09 **1 0** 09 08 07 06 05 04 03 02 01

Right side **(outward-negative) and inward-positive**

Figure.4 **First Dimension with Numbers**

The reader can notice that having a number minus ten (-10) at the center, the numbers run positive from 1 to 10 on both arms, going "inward". From 10 to 1, the numbers run negative going "outward." These arms create a line (Geometry)or the *First Dimension*. Figure.5.

It also creates:

a) The second pair of opposites (negative and positive). The first pair is Electricity and Gravity.

b) Directions: Inward and Outward, also Left and Right.

c) Motion/Vibration: The creation of each number is a pulse of energy waves.

Each number represents in Geometry a dot. The addition of dots creates a horizontal line (length). It creates the First Dimension of space as well as an orientation line. At the same time, it creates two opposite directions, east (positive)and west (negative).

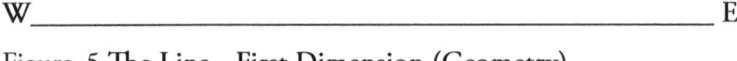

W_____ E

Figure. 5 The Line - First Dimension (Geometry)

Note: First dimension represents the second level of the inverted pyramid.

Third Invisible Minute Before the Big Bang

Minute #3 The Creation of The Cosmic Numeral Cross (CNC) The Beginning of the Invisible 2nd Dimension

Once upon a time…The Principle of Duplication and Repetition continued the process of creation. The horizontal line duplicates itself at the center point number minus (-10), the origin. It creates two lines with 4 equal arms.

One arm runs vertical from North to South, and the other arm runs horizontal from East to West, intersecting at right angles, perpendicular to each other. The intersection creates a cross, which I call *The Cosmic Numeral Cross (CNC)*

The Cosmic Numeral Cross

Figure. 6 **The Cosmic Numeral Cross without numbers**

Figure. 6A **with numbers**

<u>N</u> (360)

```
                                01
                                02
                                03
                                04
                                05
                                06
                                07
                                08
                                09
(270)W 01 02 03 04 05 06 07 08 09 1 0 09 08 07 06 05 04 03 02 01  E (90)
                                09
                                08
                                07
                                06
                                05
                                04
                                03
                                02
                                01
```

<u>S </u>(180)

The Cosmic Numeral Cross with all the numbers plugged in represents the 4 cardinal directions and their corresponding degrees that we use in a compass or a circle.

NOTE:

The Cross is the first geometrical symbol that is recorded not only in the cosmos, but in our consciousness; since the horizontal line of the cross goes right and left, it represents east (positive) and west (negative). The vertical line goes up and down. It represents north (positive) and south (negative).

The cross also creates the blueprint of the 4 cardinal directions, as well as Latitude and Longitude. These are the lines that measure distance between the Earth's hemispheres, creating an imaginary grid on the

Earth. (The Prime Meridians). Latitude represents the horizontal lines and longitude the vertical lines. The center of the cross is the blueprint of the Equator. Dividing our planet in the middle or in two hemispheres, the northern and southern hemispheres.

The Cosmic Numeral Cross (CNC) also creates 4 angles of 90° degrees each, which define an imaginary circle of a total of 360° degrees. These physical examples of the cardinal directions, latitude, longitude, and the imaginary circle are one of the many examples of the first principle, which says, *"Before any physical manifestation, it must first be conceived in the Cosmic Memory Universe."* Throughout this essay, the reader will see many different physical examples of the Cosmic Numeral Cross.

In addition, the cross represents *Motion and Interaction of energy forces. Each number of the cross vibrates, and the motion creates energy waves.* The intersection of the lines where the center of the cross meets number minus (-10) holds the four *Cosmic Energy Forces* as one Cosmic force. Gravity, Electro-Magnetism, Strong nuclear, and Weak nuclear force. The Cosmic Numeral Cross and its infinite repetition create the blueprint of space.

Note: The Cosmic Numeral Cross (CNC) represents the third level of the inverted pyramid.

Four Invisible Minutes Before the Big Bang

Minute #4 The Creation of The Cosmic QuadSpace (CQS)

The Invisible 2nd Dimension Continues

Once upon a time…The principle of duplication, repetition, and transformation applies one more time. The Cosmic Numeral Cross repeats itself to the right and to the left, up and down, simultaneously, and infinitely. This super-mega motion creates what I named the Cosmic QuadSpace, a perpetual blueprint grid of Cosmic Memory Life and Energy forces.

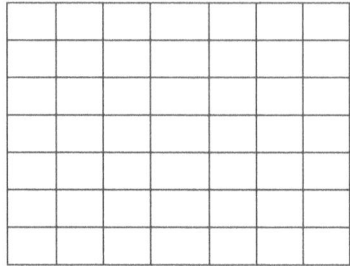

Figure. 7 **Cosmic QuadSpace (CQS)**

Note: The CosmicQuad Space represents the fourth level of the inverted pyramid.

Summary of Theory #2 and the First 4 Invisible Minutes Before the Big Bang!

The second theory, The Unity Theory and the Power of Numbers, is the theory that states that everything in the universe is interconnected, and that the cosmos is built with numbers and geometric figures beginning with the union of one (1) and zero (0), or (-10). The theory covers the first 7 minutes (**4 invisible minutes** before the Big Bang and **3 visible minutes** after the Big Bang).

Four Invisible Minutes before the Big Bang

Minute 1: Number minus ten (-10) is pure memory-energy and the unified Cosmic Force. It carries Gravity and Electricity, their union produced Electro-Magnetisms, Strong and Weak Nuclear forces.

Minute 2: First Dimension (the line). The second birth of positive and negative (inward and outward directions)

Minute 3: Invisible 2nd Dimension. The Creation of the Cosmic Numeral Cross, the source of Cosmic Memory. The cross represents the interaction of energy forces. Each number is a pulse of energy. Each number of the cross vibrates, and the motion creates energy waves.

Minute 4: Still Invisible 2nd Dimension. The Cosmic Numeral Cross repeats itself up/down, left/right infinitely, creating an invisible blueprint-grid space. The Cosmic QuadSpace. An unseen grid of Memory-Energy creates the stage for our 3rd Dimension.

In a nutshell, space is filled with invisible numbers and geometrical figures, as the reader will see throughout this essay.

Stay tuned to the next minute. The Big Bang moment!

First Visible Minute: The Big Bang Story

Minute #5 The Big Bang Story – Divided into 2 sections

(30 seconds each)

Section 1:

The Creation of Sound Energy and Transverse Waves

(30 seconds)

There was once a Big Bang Story… the Cosmic Numeral Cross (CNC) again, duplicates itself going left and right (horizontally), and back and forth, "overlapping" the CosmicQuadSpace (CQS). This rapid overlapping caused the escape of Gravity from the center of the cross number minus (-10).

This breakout caused a huge vibration between the Cosmic Numeral Cross and the CosmicQuad Space. It produced "Sound Energy." It is followed by the repetition of the Cosmic Numeral Cross (CNC), going this time up and down (vertically), perpendicular to the sound. Now, pay attention! The change of direction of the Cosmic Numeral Cross makes sound energy pass from the first dimension to the second dimension, converting sound energy into longitudinal waves (sound) and transverse waves (light).

Section 2: The Separation of Energy Forces

(Last 30 seconds of minute #5)

The first to separate from the center of the cross or number minus (-10) was Gravity, leaving behind Electromagnetism, the Strong and Weak nuclear forces. These 3 forces became the Electronuclear force. During the last 30 seconds, another separation of forces came. The first to separate from the Electronuclear force was the Strong force, followed by the Weak force and the Electromagnetic force. These 3 forces and Gravity separated and became the 4 fundamental forces that govern our universe.

This split interaction caused a radial outward ultra-super powerful cosmic energy release. I said, radial because the split of the 4 forces made the cross spin on its center causing a cosmic display of lights. "The Big Bang"

Pay attention now…The creation of longitudinal waves (Sound) and transverse waves (Light), plus the splitting off of the 4 forces (all in one minute), marks the beginning of everything that exists in our universe. Figure. 8

This is the Incredible Moment of my hypothetical

Big Bang Story!

This Photo by Unknown Author is licensed under
CC BY-NC-ND
Photo Credit: JPRALVES.NET

Figure. 8 **The Big Bang Moment**

According to Cosmologists, the beginning of our physical universe is around 13.8 billion years ago.

Second Visible Minute After the Big Bang

Minute #6 The Creation of the Visible 2nd Dimension

"The Negative and Positive Power of 2" Divided into 5 Sections: (12 seconds each.)

Once upon a time…the **Second Visible Minute** after the creation of longitudinal waves, transverse waves, and the separation of the 4 fundamental forces, or the Big Bang moment. Comes **the creation of the first physical** grid of space or the 2nd Dimension. This visible physical 2nd Dimension space overlaps the Cosmic QuadSpace(CQS).

Our physical 2nd Dimension space is the fith level of the inverted pyramid. See Figure.1.

Remember, each level is a grid system, one on top of the other in a network of dimensions. Our physical 2nd Dimension follows immediately after the Big Bang.

Section 1: The Cosmic Right Triangle

The first 12 seconds

I would like to suggest to the reader to try to see this minute with your infinite mind. All began with the first top left quadrant of the Cosmic Numeral Cross.

It creates a right triangle by running the numbers vertically from the bottom to the top, negative (-10 to 1), and from the top down positive.

Horizontally, the numbers run right to left negative, and from left to right positive, from 1 to 10. This interaction of negative and positive directions brings together an electric current field and a magnetic field.

It binds both forces together (Electricity and Magnetism) into one super force, *"Electromagnetism."* These are two sides of one coin, represented by the right triangle. Figure. 9.

Note: Space begins at ¼ of an inch. Below is a magnified right triangle so numbers can be inserted.

Figure. 9 The First Cosmic Right Triangle

									1
								1	2
							1	2	3
						1	2	3	4
					1	2	3	4	5
				1	2	3	4	5	6
			1	2	3	4	5	6	7
		1	2	3	4	5	6	7	8
	1	2	3	4	5	6	7	8	9
1	2	3	4	5	6	7	8	9	10

Section 2: The Cosmic G Square

(24 Seconds)

By fliping the right triangle to the left it creates a square. Let's call it the Cosmic G Square. G is for Gravity (gray area) Figure.10 and 11, with all the numbers plugged in.

									1
								1	2
							1	2	3
						1	2	3	4
					1	2	3	4	5
				1	2	3	4	5	6
			1	2	3	4	5	6	7
		1	2	3	4	5	6	7	8
	1	2	3	4	5	6	7	8	9
1	2	3	4	5	6	7	8	9	10

Figure. 10 **Cosmic G Square**

10	9	8	7	6	5	4	3	2	1
9	8	7	6	5	4	3	2	1	2
8	7	6	5	4	3	2	1	2	3
7	6	5	4	3	2	1	2	3	4
6	5	4	3	2	1	2	3	4	5
5	4	3	2	1	2	3	4	5	6
4	3	2	1	2	3	4	5	6	7
3	2	1	2	3	4	5	6	7	8
2	1	2	3	4	5	6	7	8	9
1	2	3	4	5	6	7	8	9	10

Figure.11 **Cosmic G Square with numbers plugged in**

The right triangle ends diagonally with number 1, the hypotenuse, which is the beginning of the opposite triangle or the virtual image of the right triangle, which represents Gravity(Gray area).

The hypotenuse keeps both triangles together. In order to separate them, an immense amount of energy is required. Electomagnetism and

Gravity are very closely related. I named it the "Electromagnetic Cosmic force."

These 24 seconds are the starting point of the structure of our 2nd Dimension and the outline of our physical space.

The First Cosmic Right Triangle is the seed of creation of the visible second dimension. All geometrical figures evolved from the right triangle. Figure.9

Let us pause for a second and go back to Pythagoras's equation. $a^2 + b^2 = c^2$

The right triangle whose angles are 45°-45°-90° and the ratio between the angles is 1:1:√2 . These two equations are the basic micro-unit to measure distance between planets, galaxies, etc. There is no need to invent another equation. ***Brilliant Pythagoras!***

Section 3: The Cosmic Isosceles Triangle and the Cosmic Rectangle (36 seconds)

Lets keep visualizing the doubling. When the Cosmic G Square flips to the top right. *Electromagnetism (white area)* ***and Gravity*** (*gray area*) create the first Cosmic Rectangle and the first Cosmic Isosceles Triangle. Figure. 12. This is another 2-in-1 creation process.

Figure. 12 **Cosmic Isosceles Triangle and the Cosmic Rectangle**

									1									
								1	2	1								
							1	2	3	2	1							
						1	2	3	4	3	2	1						
					1	2	3	4	5	4	3	2	1					
				1	2	3	4	5	6	5	4	3	2	1				
			1	2	3	4	5	6	7	6	5	4	3	2	1			
		1	2	3	4	5	6	7	8	7	6	5	4	3	2	1		
	1	2	3	4	5	6	7	8	9	8	7	6	5	4	3	2	1	
1	2	3	4	5	6	7	8	9	1 0	9	8	7	6	5	4	3	2	1

Section 4:

The Super-Cosmic G Square and the Cosmic Rhombus.

(48 Seconds of the Second Visible Minute After Big Bang.)

When the Cosmic Rectangle repeats itself to the bottom it becomes a Super Cosmic G Square and creates a new geometrical figure. The Cosmic Rhombus Figure 13.

									1									
								1	2	1								
							1	2	3	2	1							
						1	2	3	4	3	2	1						
					1	2	3	4	5	4	3	2	1					
				1	2	3	4	5	6	5	4	3	2	1				
			1	2	3	4	5	6	7	6	5	4	3	2	1			
		1	2	3	4	5	6	7	8	7	6	5	4	3	2	1		
	1	2	3	4	5	6	7	8	9	8	7	6	5	4	3	2	1	
1	2	3	4	5	6	7	8	9	10	9	8	7	6	5	4	3	2	1
	1	2	3	4	5	6	7	8	9	8	7	6	5	4	3	2	1	
		1	2	3	4	5	6	7	8	7	6	5	4	3	2	1		
			1	2	3	4	5	6	7	6	5	4	3	2	1			
				1	2	3	4	5	6	5	4	3	2	1				
					1	2	3	4	5	4	3	2	1					
						1	2	3	4	3	2	1						
							1	2	3	2	1							
								1	2	1								
									1									

Figure 13. **The Super Cosmic G Square and the Cosmic Rhombus**

> *There are 5 Cosmic geometrical shapes that make the fabric of our visible 2nd Dimension.*

The Right Triangle.
The Square.
The Isosceles Triangle.
The Rhombus.
The Rectangle.

But only the right triangle holds inside the Isosceles Triangle, the Square, and the Circle.

The Rhombus and the Rectangle are considered by-products of the square; therefore, they are not original.

NOTE:

Inside the Super Cosmic G Square Figure.13 are: 8 right triangles, 4 squares, 2 isosceles triangles, and 2 rectangles.

These repeating patterns reflect a universal principle of doubling, repetition, and transformation.

After billions of years, space might look empty, but it is full of invisible numbers, crosses, right triangles, isosceles triangles, squares, rhombuses, and rectangles. These repetitions can go up, down, right, and left infinitely. Every time it repeats, it gets bigger.

It keeps repeating infinitely and expanding forever. This fast expansion runs on the Positive Power of 2. (1,2,4,8,16,32,64…)

In this imaginary theory, our 2nd Dimension, "The Numeral Positional dimension," is a physical manifestation of the invisible CosmicQuadSpace. Our 2nd Dimension is a blend of electromagnetic and gravitational forces. However, at this stage, Gravity is a silent partner.

Gravity becomes active in our 3rd Dimension. In a capsule, the 2nd Dimension is created by repeating these 5 geometrical figures in a geometric progression of the Positive Power of 2 by doubling infinitely and expanding space forever. Except for the first inch, after one inch comes the positive Power of 2.

Do not go away, stay tuned!

Section 5: The Creation of the Cosmic Spiral Inside the Cosmic Rectangle. (Rotation)

(Last 12 seconds of the Second Visible Minute after the Big Bang.)

The Cosmic Rectangle that is inside the Cosmic G Square has the Cosmic Numeral Cross at the center of the cross (-10). It becomes the nucleus or the eye of the Cosmic Spiral.

Here, the first spiral arm of the Cosmic Spiral starts with (-10), the eye of the cosmic spiral, then goes negative around number 9. The second spiral arm goes around number 8, and the third arm goes around number 7. Followed by 6, 5, 4, 3, 2 going negatively, and in the same direction until it reaches number one.

At number 1, the spiral arm goes around positively, and in the same direction from number 1, 2, 3, 4 until it reaches number 10.

Figure. 14 **The Rotation of the Cosmic Spiral with all the Numbers Plugged-in.**

The spiral arms get bigger one row at a time, negatively and positively. This is the beginning of the spiral rotation. This process is repeated at different positions on the 2nd Dimension. Each arm of the spiral increases its distance from the center minus ten (-10), one row at a time.

In the cosmos, this process creates flat galaxies. In our physical world, Mother Nature creates seashells, sunflowers, hurricanes, tornadoes, etc.

During the rotation process, each arm is composed of rows of the same numbers. Here comes the repetition of the same numbers. One row is odd numbers and the other one is even numbers.

The rotation goes on and on forever, forming galaxies. According to the "Cool Cosmos website," there are between hundreds of billions and 2 trillion galaxies.

The Cosmic Spiral changes positions repeatedly and endlessly, creating the unborn flat spiral galaxies. It is the origin of the structure of flat spiral galaxies.

Summary of Minute #6 The Creation of the Second Physical Dimensionon

---

Minute #6 marks the creation of the Second Physical Dimension. In five phases, the Cosmic Right Triangle gives birth to a series of geometrical figures.

1. The Cosmic Right Triangle.
2. The Cosmic G Square.
3. The Cosmic Rectangle and the Cosmic Isosceles Triangle.
4. The Cosmic Rhombus
5. The Cosmic Spiral

Structure: Begins with (-10) the eye of the cosmic spiral, then the spiral arms go negatively and positively one row at a time, creating its structure and the hidden code in Mother Nature; such as sunflowers, honeycomb, and tornedos.

Rotation: Spiraling outward from the center of the Cosmic Numeral Cross. Expanding by the Power of 2. Symbolizing the ever-growing structure of space and matter.

The Second Dimension begins from invisible memory to visible matter. Creating forms and shapes.

Every form is a memory, every movement a vibration every number a position.

NOTE:

The Negative Power of 2 begins with the Cosmic Right Triangle, which is a negative fraction.

$$\left\{ \frac{1}{2}, \frac{1}{4}, \frac{1}{8}, \frac{1}{16}, \frac{1}{32}, \frac{1}{64}, \cdots \right\}$$

After the first inch begins the positive Power of 2 (1,2,4,8,16,32,64 and keeps growing forever.

The reader can imagine the 2nd Dimension as the sleeping stage of the 3rd Dimension. The physical universe awakes in a Flat 2nd Dimension called, in this imaginary theory, the "Numeral Positional Dimension."

All the matters, energies, and forces were created within the first 7 minutes: Four invisible minutes before the Big Bang, and three visible minutes after the Big Bang.

Do not go away!

Here comes the 3rd Dimension and the Last Minute of the Big Bang Story

Third Visible Minute After the Big Bang

Minute #7: The Creation of the 3rd Dimension

Let us imagine space as an organized Memory Grid System, layered with inner dimensions. (Think of the Inverted Pyramid, Figure.1. At the same time, visualize space like a brain—within this space-brain, exist dimensions with distinct functions.

Geometrically speaking, this space-brain is filled with invisible numbers, crosses, triangles, squares, rhombuses, and rectangles. These geometrical figures duplicate, repeat, and transform themselves continuously in our physical world, manifesting as stars, galaxies, planets, and more.

This repetition forms the basis of perpetual creation. All shapes are interconnected, from the first inch of the space-brain to the formation of the first atom.

Before entering the Third Dimension, let us briefly rewind to the previous dimensions:

- **Zero and First Dimension (Minute #1 and #2):** Both originate in the invisible moment before the Big Bang, beginning at a negative value of minus ten (-10)—a point or zero dimension that is the center of what will become the Cosmic Numeral Cross.

- **First Dimension:** From the zero point, or minus ten (-10), the numbers runs positive (inward) and negative (outward), creating a line or the First Dimension. It also creates the second pair of opposites, directions, motion, and vibration.

- **Minute #3 – The Second (Invisible) Dimension:** The horizontal line duplicates itself at the center point (-10), creating two lines with four equal arms. These perpendicular lines intersect to form what I call the *Cosmic Numeral Cross (CNC).* This center point holds the memory of all existence and contains the four fundamental forces: Gravity,

Electromagnetism, the Strong Nuclear Force, and the Weak Nuclear Force.

- **Minute #4 – The *CosmicQuad Space* (CQS):** This is the invisible grid that emerges from the Cosmic Numeral Cross. When the Cosmic Numeral Cross repeats itself to the right/left, up/down simultaneously, this motion creates an invisible grid, the *CosmicQuad Space. (CQS).*

- **Minute #5 – The Big Bang:** The first 30 seconds mark the creation of sound energy (longitudinal waves) and transverse waves (light). The second 30 seconds involve the separation of the fundamental energy forces. Together, this one-minute span signals the genesis of our universe. The Big Bang.

- **Minute #6 – Second Visible Dimension:** This stage introduces the formation of cosmic shapes such as right triangles, squares, rectangles, and rhombuses, all derived from the Cosmic Right Triangle and governed by the powers of 2. This expansion begins with a negative scale (from 1/16 inch to 1 inch) and then continues positively with the Power of 2 (2, 4, 8, 16, …), creating vibrations and wave motions.

The Creation of the 3rd Dimension

The Third Dimension is a by-product of the Second Dimension, just as the Second Dimension is born from the *CosmicQuad Space*, which itself arises from the *Cosmic Numeral Cross*, and so on—tracing back to the First Dimension and ultimately the Zero Dimension (minus ten, -10), or the point of cosmic memory and the origin of life.

The Third Dimension begins with an extension of the *Cosmic Numeral Cross*, where each of its four arms now expands positively from 1 to 10. Figure. 15 (Figure 15 is on page 133) This extension serves two purposes:

1. To complete the cycle of negative and positive poles.

2. To initiate the formation of the Cube, which geometrically represents **depth**, **volume**, and thus, the *Third Dimension.*

By extending the arms outward from 1 to 10, a positive parallel rhombus is formed in diagonal alignment with the original square. In this configuration. (Positive and negative parallel rhombus) The hypotenuse becomes the number 10. Figure.16 A Positive Parallel Rhombus (#10) and a Negative Cosmic Rhombus (#1) and Figure. 17 Positive and Negative Parallel Rhombus with all the numbers Plugged-In

This construction highlights the interaction of negative and positive poles—core forces of the Second Dimension: **Electromagnetism** (negative) and **Gravity** (positive).

Applying the principle of repetition, the new positive rhombus replicates itself at the center of the preceding one, overlapping each other—up, down, left, and right—creating a superimposed matrix of energy waves moving at ultra-speed. This dynamic motion further separates Electromagnetism from Gravity, elevating Gravity to the role of the **Super Cosmic G-Force**—the ruling force of the Third Dimension.

Gravity becomes the cohesive force of the universe, emerging through the repetition of rhombuses and horizontal squares, the *Super Cosmic G Square*, which reinforces its dominion, making Gravity the Mighty King of the Third Dimension.

In the Third Dimension, Electromagnetism takes on a new role—**Light**. The rhombus repeats as a square (the *Cosmic G Square*), and then alternates between parallel and square positions, expanding with each repetition.

3rd Dimension

```
                                  10
                                   9
                                   8
                                   7
                                   6
                                   5
                                   4
                                   3
                                   2
                                   1
                                   2
                                   3
                                   4
                                   5
                                   6
                                   7
                                   8
                                   9
10 9 8 7 6 5 4 3 2 1 2 3 4 5 6 7 8 9 10 9 8 7 6 5 4 3 2 1  2 3 4 5 6 7 8 9 10
                                   9
                                   8
                                   7
                                   6
                                   5
                                   4
                                   3
                                   2
                                   1
                                   2
                                   3
                                   4
                                   5
                                   6
                                   7
                                   8
                                   9
                                  10
```

Figure. 15 **Positive Extension of the Cosmic Numeral Cross**

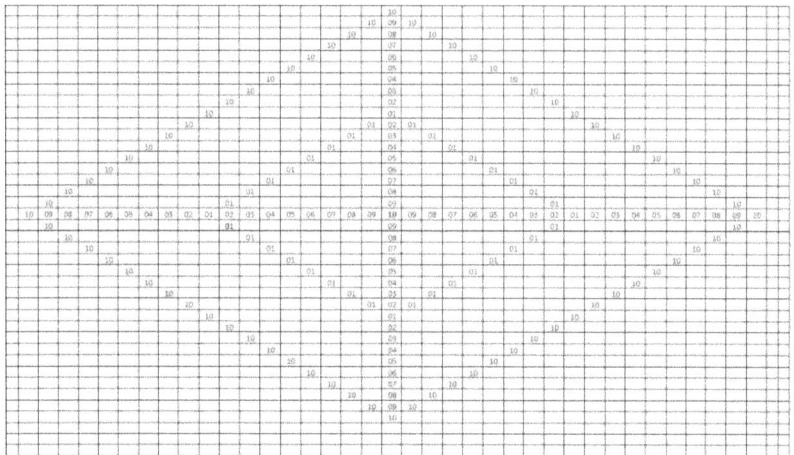

Figure. 16 – A Positive Parallel Rhombus (#10) and a Negative Cosmic Rhombus (#1)

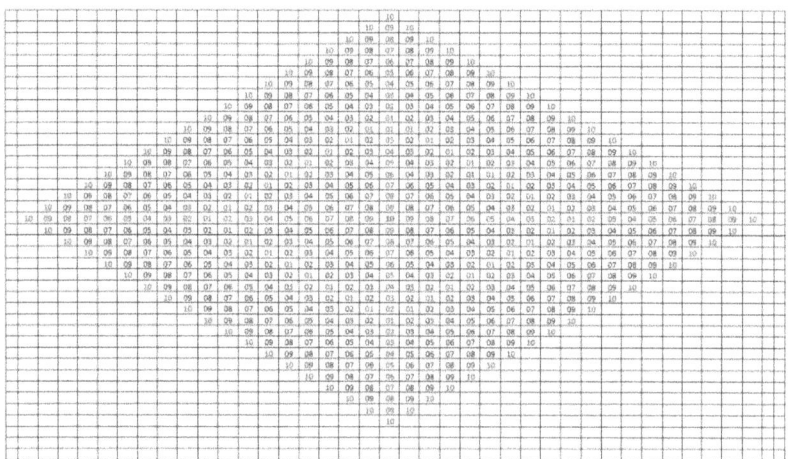

Figure. 17 Positive and Negative Parallel Rhombus with all the numbers Plugged-In

134

This infinite repetition gives birth to our three-dimensional space, which I called the Rhombic Cubic-Cross Space (RCCS) Figure 19. Through this motion Gravity manifests as the supreme force shaping our Third dimension.

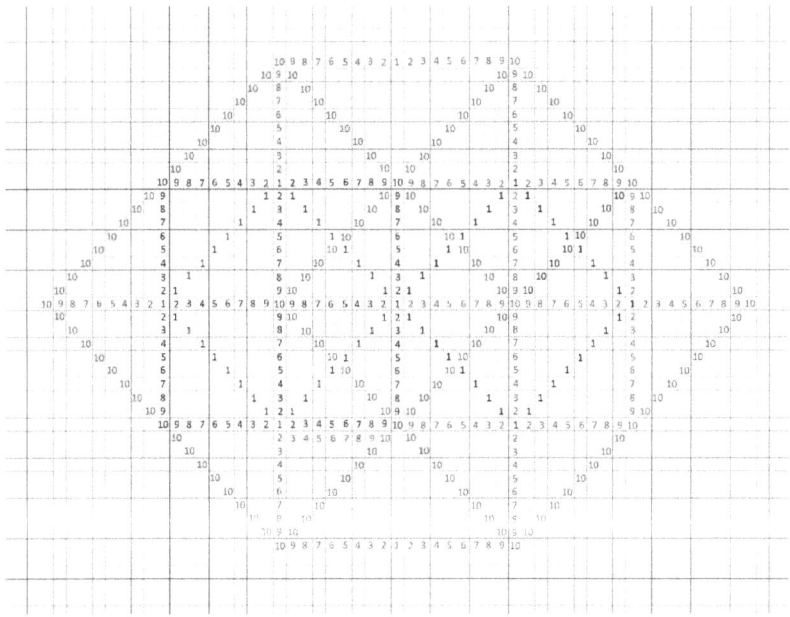

Figure. 18 **The Cube with all the numbers Plugged-In**

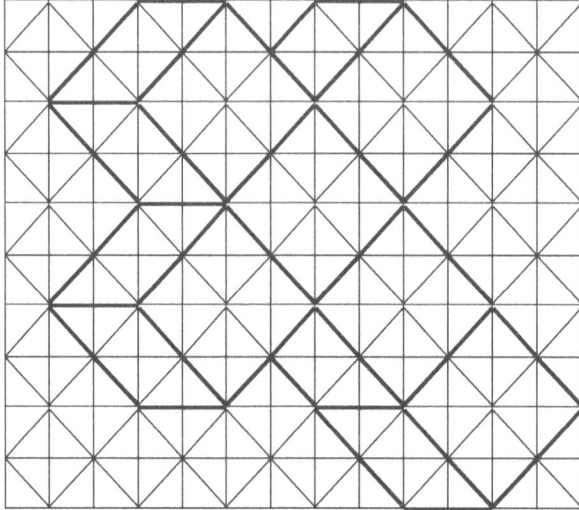

Figure. 19 **Rhombic Cubic-Cross Space (RCCS)**

Summary: Creation of the 3rd Dimension

The **Cube** emerges as an extension of the Cosmic Numeral Cross, completing the cycle of negative and positive poles. This extension initiates the formation of depth and volume—the essential attributes of the **Third Dimension.**

In this cosmic hierarchy, the **Second Dimension** is ruled by the **Electromagnetic Force**, while the **Third Dimension** is governed by **Gravity.**

The Third-Dimension manifests as a **Rhombic Cubic-Cross Space (RCCS).**

Our 3rd Dimensional Space is not empty—it is vibrantly filled with numbers, squares within squares, and geometrical layers that interweave to form the **Rhombic-Cubic Cross Space.** This is the intricate architecture of our reality.

Conclusion:

The Creation of the Universe and Our Connection to God

The **universe** is both a product of the **Big Bang** and the manifestation of **Divine Thought**. Through imagination, intuition, and insight, we begin to perceive the sacred interconnectedness of all things: space, time, energy, and matter. The Infinite and the Finite are not in opposition—they work in harmony, creating and transforming the cosmos together.

By understanding the cosmic principles of **memory**, **repetition**, and **transformation**, we begin to recognize the unity of all existence, just as the human spirit is inseparable from the Divine. This awareness awakens us to our own divine essence and our profound relationship with the **Cosmic Consciousness**.

The universe was conceived in the **Mind of God**. This is why the laws of nature are not random but deeply encoded with **Memory-Energy**, or what we may call **Divine Consciousness**.

Extra Bonus

The Creation Story in Seven Minutes

In the stillness before time began, there was only a One and a Zero—whistling through the breath of the wind, carried on the sound of creation itself. A voice rose from the deep: *"I AM THE VERB," the Living Word.* The One and the Zero must not be separated, but are two faces of one eternal number. Minus Ten—a single, concentrated point holding all cosmic memory and energy, infinite and indivisible.

On the second day, from the heart of Minus Ten, the point began to extend—duplicating to the right and to the left—from that motion, an invisible horizon appeared. The second duality was born: the polarity of positive and negative. Two forces intertwined, birthing motion, direction, and vibration. Each number became a pulse of memory-energy, carrying the essence of creation.

On the third day, the horizon reflected itself again, this time rising vertically through the center of Minus Ten. From this reflection emerged a sacred cross—the *Cosmic Numeral Cross*—a radiant intersection, an axis of memory, energy, time, and the first breath of space itself. It marked the intersection where the infinite touched the finite.

On the fourth day, the winds whispered, "The Cross must not stand still." And so, it leapt joyfully, shifting up and down, right and left, without end. Through this motion, the blueprint of the second dimension took shape, the *CosmicQuad Space,* an eternal and unseen grid pulsing with memory-energy, preparing the dance of creation.

On the fifth day, the voice of creation echoed once more, now resonating with deeper power: *"I AM THE VERB. I AM THE LIGHT."* With those words, sound and light burst into existence. United in a divine dance of becoming. The primordial energy forces split into four Cosmic Dancers, each moving in rhythm, setting time into motion. Light exploded into color, color into form, and form into life, illuminating the vast space with sacred brilliance. *The birth of Creation.*

On the sixth day, the invisible Mind of the Cosmos—the living Word, the eternal "I AM"—began shaping the newborn second dimension. The Cosmic Right Triangle appeared, the first sacred seed of geometry. Its mirrored reflections gave birth to the Cosmic Square, the Isosceles Triangle, the Rectangle, the Rhombus, and finally the Cosmic Spiral. Each one multiplied by the sacred power of two. Each a whisper of infinity echoing into the finite. Every form held memory; every vibration carried the signature of the Living Cosmic God.

On the seventh day, space danced—the dance of creation. The Cube emerged from the heart of the Cosmic Numeral Cross, completing the cycle of positive and negative. A positive diagonal Rhombus unfolded, shifting into a Square, and through infinite repetition, the third dimension was born. *The Rhombic-Cube-Cross Space*—an intricate living architecture where all things could become—The breath of life swept over it all, and the wind whispered once more: *"I AM THE VERB,"* said the voice, the Living Word. *"I AM THE LIGHT."*

EIGHT STEPS: THE CREATION OF THE UNIVERSE (Inch by Inch)

Step One:

The birth of our physical universe started at ¼ of an inch with the Cosmic Numeral Cross to be. ✚ horizontally and vertically. Since the size is too small, I cannot compress the numbers from 10 to 1.

The next step started with the left quadrant of the cross at ¼ of an inch. One leg that is ¼ inch horizontally. One leg is ¼ inch vertically.

MAGNIFIED

									1
								1	2
							1	2	3
						1	2	3	4
					1	2	3	4	5
				1	2	3	4	5	6
			1	2	3	4	5	6	7
		1	2	3	4	5	6	7	8
	1	2	3	4	5	6	7	8	9
1	2	3	4	5	6	7	8	9	10

REAL
SIZE

Cosmic Right Triangle

Step Two

When the Cosmic Right Triangle flips to **the top left,** it becomes The Cosmic G Square. Real size: (¼ of an inch on 4 sides.)

MAGNIFIED

									1
								1	2
							1	2	3
						1	2	3	4
					1	2	3	4	5
				1	2	3	4	5	6
			1	2	3	4	5	6	7
		1	2	3	4	5	6	7	8
	1	2	3	4	5	6	7	8	9
1	2	3	4	5	6	7	8	9	10

REAL SIZE

Cosmic G Square

Step Three:

When the Cosmic G Square moves to the top right, it creates the Cosmic Isosceles Triangle and the Cosmic Rectangle.

MAGNIFIED

									1									
								1	2	1								
							1	2	3	2	1							
						1	2	3	4	3	2	1						
					1	2	3	4	5	4	3	2	1					
				1	2	3	4	5	6	5	4	3	2	1				
			1	2	3	4	5	6	7	6	5	4	3	2	1			
		1	2	3	4	5	6	7	8	7	6	5	4	3	2	1		
	1	2	3	4	5	6	7	8	9	8	7	6	5	4	3	2	1	
1	2	3	4	5	6	7	8	9	1 0	9	8	7	6	5	4	3	2	1

REAL SIZE

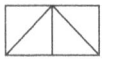

The Cosmic Isosceles Triangle and the Cosmic Rectangle.

Real size: (¼ an inch vertically and ½ inch horizontally)

Step Four:

When the Cosmic Rectangle repeats itself at the bottom, it becomes a Super Cosmic G Square and creates a new geometrical figure. *The Cosmic Rhombus.* Space is still at ½ of an inch on all 4 sides.

MAGNIGIED

The Super Cosmic G Cosmic Square and the Cosmic Rhombus.

Real size: (½ inch on all sides of the square.)

								1										
							1	2	1									
						1	2	3	2	1								
					1	2	3	4	3	2	1							
				1	2	3	4	5	4	3	2	1						
			1	2	3	4	5	6	5	4	3	2	1					
		1	2	3	4	5	6	7	6	5	4	3	2	1				
	1	2	3	4	5	6	7	8	7	6	5	4	3	2	1			
1	2	3	4	5	6	7	8	9	8	7	6	5	4	3	2	1		
1	2	3	4	5	6	7	8	9	10	9	8	7	6	5	4	3	2	1
	1	2	3	4	5	6	7	8	9	8	7	6	5	4	3	2	1	
		1	2	3	4	5	6	7	8	7	6	5	4	3	2	1		
			1	2	3	4	5	6	7	6	5	4	3	2	1			
				1	2	3	4	5	6	5	4	3	2	1				
					1	2	3	4	5	4	3	2	1					
						1	2	3	4	3	2	1						
							1	2	3	2	1							
								1	2	1								
									1									

REAL SIZE

Note:

Steps five to eight are the real size with no numbers

Step Five:

REAL SIZE THE COSMIC RECTANGLE

Again, the Super Cosmic G Square, which is ½ inch on 4 sides of the square. It repeats to the right. It becomes a Rectangle of 1 inch horizontally and ½ inch vertically.

Step Six:

The Cosmic Rectangle repeats at the **bottom.** It becomes a square of 1 inch on 4 sides of the square.

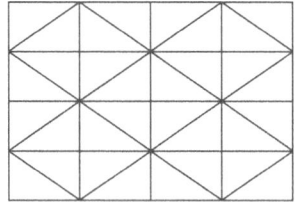

Notice *that a 2nd second-dimensional diagonal Cross and a fifth Rhombus emerged at the center.*

Step Seven:

Again, the square that is 1 inch on 4 sides of the square, repeats to the right and becomes a bigger rectangle of 2 inches horizontally and 1 inch vertically. Creating what I called *the Carpenter's Square,* interlacing each other in opposite directions. (The origin of waves)

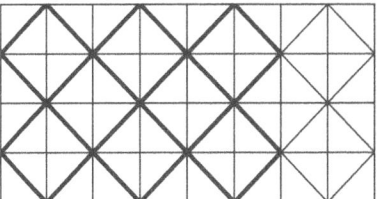

Carpenter's Square/And a bigger Rhombus

The interlocking creates a *bigger Rhombus* at the center of the carpenter's square with 4 rhombuses inside it.

The rectangle grows after the first inch by the power of 2. The bigger it gets, the more empty space our mortal eyes see. But in reality, space is full of geometrical shapes and numbers.

Step 8 Third Dimension (The Cube)

When the Cosmic Rectangle repeats to the bottom, it becomes 2 inches horizontally and 2 inches vertically. Creating the Cube (volume) and the third dimension.

At the same time, creating the Rhombic Cubic-Cross Space, which is the blueprint of the Third Dimension.

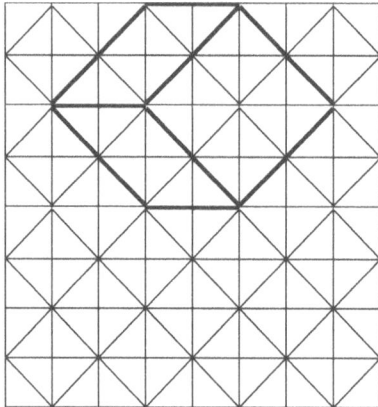

The Cube

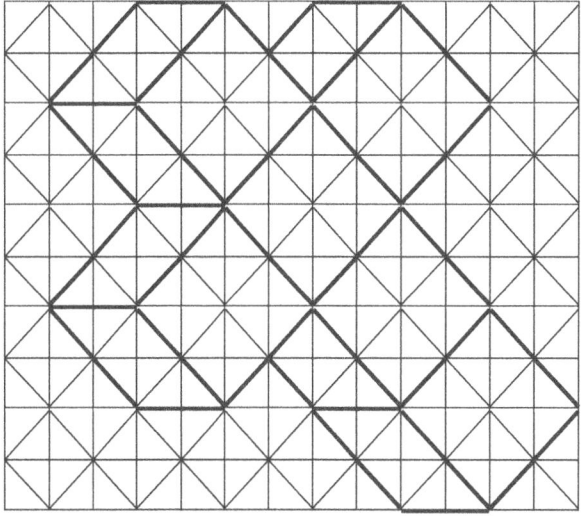

Rhombic Cubic-Cross Space (RCCS)

THE END OF THE IMAGINATION!

BONUS

PROSE
OF
GOD

WHO IS GOD?

God is Light.
God is Good.

God is Harmony.
God is Order.

God is One.
God is the Creator.

God is Universal.
God is Consciousness.

God is Energy.
God is Truth.

God is Intelligence.
God is Infinite.

God is Love.
God is ALL!

DISTORTION OF GOD

Birth and death are handed to us.
Norms and values are instilled in us.
God, religion, and faith are presented as truths.

"If you do this or that, God will punish you."
"If someone dies, it is God's will."

Can God be so conflicted, so cruel?
This is the God we were introduced to—
a God twisted by society, distorting our beliefs.

As children, we believe in God.
As teenagers, we reject God.
As adults, we doubt God.

Did God exist, or was it just a myth, a legend?
I thought I knew God. I was wrong.
I thought I knew myself. I was wrong.

It took me years—life after life—
to consciously understand God,
to glimpse my true self and the true God.

How long will it take you?

I AM. YOU ARE. A Spiritual Being.
Can we consciously alter our destiny?
Or is our destiny pre-designed—perhaps by us, perhaps by God?

A masterpiece of the evolution of self—
where time does not exist,
where harmony prevails,
where God is ALL that exists.

THE JOY OF DEATH

Do not feel sad, do not feel sorry.
Do not cry. I AM ALIVE.

I AM!

I am not my body, I have had many of them.
Each one vanished under the shadow of time.

Many times, I was a man, a woman, fat or thin.
I was black, white, mulatto, rich, or poor.
I was married, single, gay, or transgender.
I was Catholic, an Atheist, Jewish, Baptist, and Buddhist
I was paralyzed, handicapped, or healthier.

All nations were my country.
All races were my race.
All religions were my belief.

I was learning to love through many bodies.
I was learning to love through many races.
I was learning to love through every life experience.
I was learning to consciously recognize my presence.

I AM!

I AM NOT MY BODY. I AM ALIVE!
I AM, is the essence of self.
I AM, is the verb of life

I AM ALIVE!

*   **This poem is dedicated to my family, friends, and special*
people in my life

OUR DESTINY

God is Air. God is Fire. God is Water.
Our destiny is to feel the air.
To witness the flame. To drink the water.

God is Earth. God is Energy. God is Love.
Our destiny is to perceive the rhythm of the earth.
To transform energy and to give love.

God is the Cosmic Mind. God is Truth.
Our destiny is to perceive our thinking.
To listen deeply and to know the truth.

God is Intelligence. God is Light.
Our destiny is to be one with the intelligence.
And to feel the inner light.

God is Love. God is the Creator!
Our destiny is to become co-creators.
To shape and transform our life.
.

God is a Cosmic Consciousness. God is All!
Our destiny is to remember who we are.
We are ONE with the Cosmic Mind.

WE ARE CREATORS

The mind creates good and evil.
There is no heaven or hell.
The mind creates heaven.
The mind creates hell.

We are Creators!

Do not blame God for your failure.
Do not praise God for your success.
God has nothing to do with your choices.
You reward or punish yourself.

It is the principle of Cause and Effect!

"Free Will" is your last name.
Disregard the God that you know.
Society distorted its image for its purpose.
Choose to "consciously" recognize God.

God will reveal to you! God is Perfect!

DUST OF TRUTH

1. Do not search for God in a synagogue or cathedral.
God lives inside your heart!
We are unconscious temples of God!

2. Our ignorance of the truth makes us unbelievers.
We must make a "conscious" connection with God.
It's time to wake up and begin the search.

3. God's universe is peace, love, and harmony
Not war, hate, or chaos.

4. We create war, we perpetuate hate, racism and bigotry
Why?, Why, Why?

When we can choose peace and friendship.
To respect one another's differences.
Why Not? Why Not? Why Not?

GOD IS.....

To the Egyptian... God is "The Sun RA"
To the Muslims... God is "Allah"

To the Jewish... God is "Yahweh"
To the Hindu... God is "Brahman"

To the Christian... God is "Jesus Christ"
To the Atheist... there is no God

Many religions teach us what God is.
However, God is not a religion.

Religion is society's invention.
God is Infinite love, God is Life!

God is the Universal Father!
God is the Universal Mother!

God is Cosmic Consciousness!
God is Light! God is ALL!

PERCEPTION OF DEATH

First perception: Five years old
Walking with my mother in the old neighborhood.
I heard people crying. I looked at the blue house.
A black coffin stood in the middle of the living room.

"Someone died," my mother said.

I wanted to run, to disappear. I was frightened!
Eternal seconds passed through my little brain.
The image of death etched itself into my mind.

Second perception: Thirteen years old
My friend's mother died. I was afraid!
My cousin and I went to the wake.
Again, the black coffin loomed in my memory.

I stood at a distance, staring at the wooden box.
My stomach roared like an earthquake.

"Let's pay our respects," my cousin said.

I wanted to run. I wanted to disappear.
My stomach became a volcano.
I was scared! My hands were sweating!
Endless seconds passed through my body.
The image of death burned into my mind.

Third perception: Twenty-eight years old
My grandmother died—my first personal loss.
Both images of death resurfaced in my memory.
This time, I was not afraid. Instead, I asked God:

Life cannot end in a coffin!

I began to search and search...
I found a puzzle of perceptions and reality,
A mixture of knowledge and insight.

I realized that the essence of self is not the body.
I realized there is no death.

The spirit is our true self.
We are ageless spiritual creatures.
We are the timeless whisper of life.

Interminable seconds passed through my heart.
The image of death dissolved from my mind.
I Am Free!

PERCEPTION OF THE MIND

Perception is not reality.
Emotions and thoughts are one!
Revolving inside the mind.
Cluster of energy and vibrations.
Entire body is composed of many parts.
Physical, emotional, mental, and spiritual
Theories of science blend with legends
Inertia of the past. Chaos of the mind!
Old thoughts engraved in our minds.
Nothing exists without creation!

Original thought of the Cosmic Mind.
Free Will is our birthright!

The first sound was the word "I AM"
History repeats itself.
Energy is the thought of creation.

Magnificent is the sound of conception.
I AM is the infinite echo!
New perception of the universe.
Double of opposite is our nature!

PERCEPTION OF LIFE

Play, sing, laugh, and jump
Enjoy each and every day
Relax, meditate, and breathe
Celebrate your birthday
Ego and vanity are,
Punishment of the soul
Twilight of one emotion
Inconsistency of the mind
Ongoing war of the senses
New consciousness of self is in the air!.

Oneness with nature is the victory
Find the way to conquer the ego

Long is the road of self-evolution
Infinite is the world of the soul
Follow your instinct, intuition, and insights.
Elevate your Self-Consciousness! I AM!

SIX WAYS TO DEAL WITH DEATH

FIRST

Accept death as part of life.

SECOND

Read how other cultures deal with death.

THIRD

Review your own concept of death.

FOURTH

Detach yourself from material things.

FIFTH

Prepare yourself for your own death.

SIXTH

Do not be afraid.
You will come back again!

THE SOURCE

The source of all life's existence.

Is the Cosmic God.

The source of all numbers.

Is Number 1.

The source of all geometrical figures.

Is a Right triangle.

The source of all physical matter.

Is Energy force!

The source of all energy force.

Is The Thought of God!

ALL IS ONE

All is the Creator.

ALL is the Source of Life.

ALL is Harmony.

ALL is Truth and Justice.

ALL is the Unity that Unite US!

ALL is ONE.

ONE is ALL.

We are ALL ONE!

PRAYER

Q & A

Q: How do people pray?
A: Not consistently. Not with Awareness.

Q: When do people pray?
A: Often only when we are in trouble.
  Often, when we are in need.

Daily Tips on How to Pray:

- *Find a quiet, consistent place to pray.*
- *Pray twice a day - morning and night.*
- *Be alone in silence.*
- *Let go of all thoughts and future thoughts.*
- *Bring that silence to God.*
- *Recognized God's presence in your heart.*
- *Feels God's love, and senses the unity of all things.*

Daily Active Prayer:

- *Begin your day without worries, fears, or envy.*
- *Be grateful and give Thanks to God.*
- *Offer hope to those who have lost faith.*
- *Lend a hand to those in need.*
- *Keep only goodness in your heart.*
- *And tomorrow, do the same.*

  Amen!

THE INTERPRETER

The brain interprets our body.
I interpret my life.

You interpret your life.
We interpret reactions!

The brain constantly interprets messages.
Messages from our nervous system.

Messages from our emotions.
Messages from our minds.

The brain receives signals and acts.
Be aware of what you think and feel.

Consciously change the message.
The interpretation will change.

The brain is the interpreter.
We are the messenger!

GOD BLESS MY BROTHERS

God bless your life.
God bless your love.

God bless the tree,
sheltering its leaves.

God bless my brothers.
A gift from God!

God bless the rain,
feeding the grass.

God bless my brothers.
Wherever they are.

God bless the sun.
Warming our hearts.

God bless the river,
embracing the lake.

God bless my brothers.
Both live in my heart.

God bless my brothers.
God bless!

I THINK OF GOD

I think of God—
when the sun warms my skin,
when morning light awakens me,
when the wind whispers against my face.

I think of God.
Yet, who is the one who thinks?

"I AM," I reply.

The wind lifts a flower to me,
its petals trembling with truth.

"You have answered yourself: 'I AM.'
You are the echo of creation,
the voice the 'I' has forgotten."

APPENDIX

APPENDIX A

POUTPOURRI OF POSITIVE AFFIRMATIONS

Affirmations serve as powerful messengers to the subconscious mind. The key objectives of this practice are:

1. **Desire to Change** – Cultivate a genuine willingness to transform.

2. **Shift Negativity to Positivity** – Replace limiting thoughts with empowering beliefs.

By committing to these objectives, you have already completed 30% of the work. The remaining 70% consists of:

- **Repeating Affirmations Consciously** – Speak them aloud with clarity.

- **Repeating with Confidence** – Reinforce them consistently.

- **Believing in Their Truth** – Internalize and trust the words you say.

- **Practicing Patience** – Growth takes patience, and time; repetition is key.

- **Alignment** – Align behaviors with affirmations to solidify change.

You can also create your own affirmations. Always write them in the present tense, keeping them short and personally meaningful.

POTPOURRI OF POSITIVE AFFIRMATIONS

"I" Affirmations

- I feel confident in myself.
- I make conscious decisions.
- I give myself permission to be free and happy.

- I trust and feel good about myself.
- I inhale life and exhale stress and tension.
- I follow my intuition.
- I bless my immune system.
- I remain calm under pressure.
- I live fully in the present moment.
- I have a healthy body and mind.
- I focus on my goals.
- I visualize my goals daily.
- I accomplish my goals.
- I embrace my new life.
- I eat mindfully.
- I consistently repeat my affirmations.

"I AM" Affirmations

- I am blessed 24/7.
- I am in control of my life.
- I am creating a new habit: _____ (fill in the blank).
- I am consciously in charge of my choices.
- I am mindful f my thoughts.
- I am pure energy, radiating light.
- I am aware of all my decisions.

"TODAY" Affirmations

- Today, I choose happiness.
- Today, I choose kindness and compassion.
- Today, I release worries and fears.
- Today, I listen attentively.
- Today marks the beginning of my new life.
- Today, I perform a good deed.

"MISCELLANEOUS" Affirmations

- Ideas and insights flow easily to me.
- When I need something, it comes to me effortlessly.
- All my needs are met.
- Helping others brings me joy.
- Patience is natural for me.
- Self-discipline is my strength.
- Exercising makes me feel great.
- I release my old self.
- I feel free, strong, and renewed.
- My mind is full of positive intentions.
- My immune system recognizes and eliminates harmful bacteria.
- My immune system works for me 24/7.
- My immune system functions in harmony with my body.
- My immune system protects me from illness and infection.
- My intention today is happiness.
- My goal is to create the best version of myself.

Final Thought

By incorporating these affirmations into your daily routine, you reinforce a mindset of positivity and self-empowerment. Believe in the process, trust yourself, and embrace the transformation.

APPENDIX B

THE 3-6-9 BREATHING & RELAXATION EXERCISES

Managing Stress Through Mindful Practices

At some point in life, we all experience stress. Often, these moments catch us off guard. Can we avoid the everyday challenges that impact our well-being, whether at home, work, or in relationships? While stress, tension, and emotional struggles can weaken the immune system and lead to conditions such as high blood pressure, headaches, and ulcers, the good news is that *we have the power to manage them.*

One of the most effective tools at our disposal is **our own thoughts**. Many of us unconsciously speak in negative terms, reinforcing stress. Statements like:

- *"Today is not my day."*
- *"I'm stuck in my job."*
- *"I have a problem with my weight."*
- *"I never seem to catch a break."*
- *"I don't know what's wrong with me today."*

These thoughts shape our reality, programming us for negativity. **But we can change that!** Each time you catch yourself thinking negatively, immediately replace that thought with a positive one. (See Appendix A for positive affirmations.)

By learning to **control negative thinking**, we close the door to stress and tension and open the door to relaxation and inner peace. This appendix provides two simple yet powerful exercises. The **3-6-9 Breathing Exercise** helps to strengthen the lungs and improve oxygen flow to the brain. In the **Relaxation Exercise,** you will find yourself in a state of tranquility.

When you practice these two exercises regularly, with attention and consistency, your lungs and heart will be stronger, and stress will fade away. It will only take you 6 to 9 minutes every day. I think it is worth trying.

The 3-6-9 Breathing Exercise

Find a comfortable position—sitting is ideal, but lying down works too. Whether alone or in a group, allow yourself to settle in.

1. **Begin with 3 breaths:** Inhale and exhale slowly through your nostrils. On the third breath, take a deep inhale, expanding your diaphragm, and hold for a count of **6**.
2. **Always exhale slowly and gently through your mouth**, maintaining a steady rhythm.
3. **Stay present and focused**—PAY ATTENTION to the sensation of breathing.
4. **Repeat this process 9 times**, allowing your mind to quiet and your body to relax.

This simple yet powerful exercise improves patience, sharpens focus, and clears intrusive thoughts. Asyou count to six, you intentionally shift your awareness, promoting inner peace while strengthening your lungs, heart, and brain.

Relaxation Exercise (30 Minutes)

Find a quiet space where you can truly unwind. Sit comfortably, close your eyes, and embrace stillness. Ignore external sounds.

- Take a deep breath, repeating the **3-6-9 Breathing Exercise** three times.
- Begin a **countdown from five to one.**
- Softly affirming with each number.
- **Five:** *My body is at ease.*
- **Four:** *I feel calm and centered.*
- **Three:** *Peace surrounds me.*
- **Two:** *I am deeply relaxed.*
- **One:** *I am completely at rest.*

- If relaxation feels incomplete, repeat the countdown until you reach full tranquility.

- Once deeply relaxed, **recite affirmations**—choose three meaningful statements and repeat each one six times.

- Pause in silence. Allow yourself to simply be.

- When ready to close the session, count upward from **one to five**, reinforcing positive thoughts.

When ready to close the session, count upward from **one to five**, reinforcing positive thoughts:

   o **One:** *I am relaxed and calm.*

   o **Two:** *I feel good within myself.*

   o **Three:** *My thoughts are under my control.*

   o **Four:** *I rise above challenges with strength.*

   o **Five:** *I embrace life with kindness and confidence.*

Slowly open your eyes. Carry this feeling of peace with you throughout your day.

This relaxation exercise is a form of **self-hypnosis**, guiding your mind toward clarity and empowerment. With consistency, relaxation will become second nature, allowing you to reclaim control over your emotions and well-being. By controlling your thoughts, your emotions obey. Practice regularly and with consistency...the Victory will be yours!

Final Thoughts

With consistent practice, these exercises will help you regain control over your thoughts, emotions, and well-being. Relaxation is not a luxury—it is a necessity for a balanced life. *Make time for yourself. Breathe. Relax. And step into a world of Peace and Tranquility.*

APPENDIX C

RESCUE ME PLAN
ESSAY 1 SNAP SHOT OF LOVE

PAGE 1 OF 2

COLUMN #1	COLUMN #2	COLUMN #3	COLUMN #4
What Positive Emotions Decreased or are gone?	What Positive Emotions Stayed or Increased?	Why and What contributed to failure?	What Happened to Cause the Decrease of loving acts?

MY ACTION PLAN

I AM MY THERAPIST! AND HERE IS MY PLAN

PAGE 2 OF 2

APPENDIX D

10 ACTIONS STEPS TO GET RID OF BAD HABITS

1. **Make Conscious Decisions**
   Never make decisions impulsively or when emotionally overwhelmed. Take a step back, assess the situation, and choose with intention.

2. **Identify & Prioritize Habits to Change**
   Write down the habits you want to eliminate. Prioritize the top three and start with the most urgent or impactful one.

3. **Create a Realistic Action Plan**
   Develop a step-by-step plan to replace the habit. Seek support from a friend to stay on track.

4. **Take Small, Consistent Steps**
   Break your goal into smaller, achievable milestones with realistic timeframes. Small wins build momentum.

5. **Master Relaxation Techniques**
   Stress often fuels bad habits. Learn deep breathing, meditation, or other relaxation methods to regain control. (Appendix B)

6. **Reinforce with Positive Affirmations**
   Use empowering affirmations to rewire your mindset. Say them daily with confidence. (Appendix A)

7. **Replace the Bad Habit with a Positive One**
   Instead of simply quitting, substitute it with a beneficial habit—exercise, start a productive morning routine, or a creative hobby.

8. **Visualize Success & Track Progress**
   Picture yourself free from the habit. Keep a log to identify patterns, recognize progress, and refine your approach.
9. **Reward Milestones**
   Set up a system to celebrate your progress—treat yourself to something enjoyable when you reach a goal.
10. **Commit with Patience, Discipline, and Persistent**
    Breaking habits takes time. Stay patient, practice self-discipline, and take consistent action. If you slip, do not give up.

TIP:

Please note that to understand why you engage in any habit. Is it stress, boredom, or social influence? Like social media, remove apps from your home screen or set app limits. **Awareness is the first step to change.**

Below are some affirmations to support your efforts. (For more affirmations, see Appendix A) These are some universal affirmations, but you can create your own. An affirmation statement depends on the habit you are trying to get rid of. Always write affirmations in the present tense.

- I HAVE PATIENCE WITH MYSELF
- PATIENCE IS MY STRENGTH
- I HAVE SELF-DISCIPLINE
- I AM RESPONSIBLE FOR MY ACTIONS
- I CONSCIOUSLY CONTROL MY THOUGHTS
- I CONSCIOUSLY CONTROL MY FEELINGS
- I AM IN HARMONY WITH MY THOUGHTS
- I AM IN HARMONY WITH MY EMOTIONS
- I AM IN HARMONY WITH MYSELF
- I AM MY OWN CREATION
- I AM PART OF THE CREATOR'S MIND
- I AM THE MASTER OF MY LIFE

What if and only if
You and I are a Thought of God

ENDNOTES

Essay #1 Snapshot of Love

1 **Subconscious:** describes something that is just below your awareness-(Vocabulary.com)

2 **Conscious:** When you do something consciously, you do it on purpose, after thinking seriously about it. (Vocabulary.com)

3 **Universal-Life-Force:** describes something for everything or everyone. In biology is a hypothetical force (not physical or chemical) once thought by Henri Bergeson to cause the evolution and development of organism. (Vocabulary.com)

4 **Generation** X, (anyone born between 1965 and 1980), the Millennials of our planet and its future.(born between 1981 and 1996), Generation Z (born between 1997 and 2012), and Alpha generation born between 2013 and 2025. (Vocabulary.com)

5 **Narcissist** – Someone who is excessively self-centered-(Vocabulary.com)

Essay #2 Snapshot of Self

1 **Free Will** made or done freely or of one's own accord; voluntary. (Dictionary.com)

2 **Cause and Effect**- Noting a relationship between actions or events such that one or more are the result of the other or others. (Dictionary.com)

3 **Karma** in Theosophy, the cosmic principle according to which each person is rewarded or punished in one incarnation according to that person's deeds in the previous incarnation. (Dictionary.com)

Essay#3 Snapshot of the Mind

1 **Conscious Mind** a) The quality or state of being aware especially of something within oneself b) The state or fact of being conscious of an external object, state, or fact c) awareness. (merriam-webster.com)

2 **Subconscious Mind** The mental activities just below the threshold of consciousness. (merriam-webster.com)

3 **Super-Conscious Mind** Transcending human or normal consciousness. (merriam-webster.com)

Essay#4 Snapshot of God and the Universe

1 **Periodic Table** – is a tabular array of the chemical elements organized by atomic number, from the element with the lowest atomic number, hydrogen, to the element with the highest atomic number, Oganesoon. (Britanica.com)

2 **The Big Bang Theory** A theory in astronomy: the universe originated billions of years ago in a rapid expansion from a single point of nearly infinite energy density. (merriam-webster.com)

3 **Pythagoras** Greek philosopher and mathematician who proved the Pythagorean theorem, considered to be the first true mathematician (circa 580-500 BC) (Vocabulary.com)

4 **Pythagorean theorem** a theorem in geometry: the square of the length of the hypotenuse of a right triangle equals the sum of the squares of the lengths of the other two sides (merriam-webster,com)

Reference/Bibliography Books

GOD

_____Aczel, A. D. (1999). God's Equation: Einstein, Relativity, and the Expanding Universe. New York, N.Y. MJF Books.

_____Benz, A. (2000). The Future of the Universe: Chance, Chaos, God? New York, NY. The Continuum Publishing Group, Inc.

_____Braden, G. (2004). *The God Code: The Secret of Our Past, the Promise of Our Future.* Carlsbad, Ca. Hay House, Inc.

_____Clegg, B.(2006). The God Effect: Quantum, Entanglement, Science's Strangest Phenomenon. New York. St. Martin's Press.

_____Connor, J.A. (2006), Pascal's Wager: The Man Who Played Dice with God. New York, N.Y Harper Collins Publishers.

_____Davies P. (1983).*God and the New Physics.* New York, N.Y. Simon & Schuster.

_____Hawking, S. (2005). God Created the Integers: The Mathematical Breakthroughs that Changed History. Edited by Stephen Hawking. Philadelphia, PA. Running Press Books Publishers.

_____Kaku, M. (2021). The God Equation: The Quest For a Theory of Everything. New York. Double Day.

_____Livio, M. (2009). *Is God a Mathematician?* New York, N.Y. Simon & Schuster.

PHYSICS/MATHEMATICS/SCIENCE/HISTORY

_____Aczel, A.D. (1996). Fermat's Last Theorem: Unlocking the Secret of an Ancient Mathematical Problem. New York, NY A Delta Book, Dell Publishing

_____Alder, K. (2002). The Measure of Things: The Seven Year Odyssey and Hidden Error that Transformed the World. New York, NY. Free Press.

_____Barbour, J. (2020). The Janus Point: A New Theory of Time. New York, NY Basic Books.

_____Barrow, J.D. (2007). New Theories of Everything: The Quest for Ultimate Explanations. New York, NY. Oxford University Press.

_____Bartusiak, M. (2000). Einstein's Unfinished Symphony: Listen to the Sound of Space and Time. New York. NY. Berkley Books.

_____Charap, J.M. (2002). Explaining the Universe: The New Age of Physics. Princeton, N.J. Princeton University Press.

_____Crease, R.P. (2008). The Great Equations: Breakthroughs in Science from Pythagoras to Heisenberg. New York. W.W. Norton and Company, Inc.

_____Derbyshire, J. (2004). Prime Obsession: Bernhard Riemann and the Greatest Unsolved Problems in Mathematics. Washington DC. Plume Books.

_____Dixon, R. (1991). Mathographics. Mineola, NY. Dover Publications, Inc.

_____Ferguson, K. (1991). *Stephen Hawking. Quest for a Theory of Everything.* New York. Bantam Books.

_____Ferguson, K. (2008) The Music of Pythagoras. New York, NY. Walker and Company.

_____Feyman, R.P. (1995). Six Easy Pieces: Essentials of Physics Explained by Its Most Brilliant Teacher. New York, NY. Perseus Books.

_____Fuller, M. (2002). Building Materials for Life. Macon, GA. Smyth & Helwys Publishing, Inc.

_____Gamow G. (2002). Gravity. Mineola, New York. Dover Publication, Inc.

_____Heath, R. (2011). Precessional Time and the Evolution of Consciousness.: How Stories Create the World. Rochester, Vermont. Inner Traditions.

_____Heisenberg, W. (1949)The Physical Principles of the Quantum Theory. New York, NY. Dover Publication, Inc.

_____Hossenfelder, S. (2022).Existential Physics: A Scientist's Guide to Life's Biggest Questions. New York, NY. Vikings,

_____Joos, G. and Freeman, I.M. (1986)Theoretical Physics. New Y0ork. Dover Publications. Inc.

_____Kaplan, R. & Kaplan, E. (2003). The Art of the Infinite: The Pleasures of Mathematics. New York, NY. Oxford University Press.

_____Kirkland, K. (2007) Force and Motion. New York, N.Y Facts on File, Inc.

_____Kirkland, K. (2007) Light and Optics. New York, N.Y Facts on File, Inc.

_____Kline, M. (1967). Mathematics for the Nonmathematician. New York. Dover Publications.

_____Murchie, G. (1981). Then Seven Mysteries of Life: Exploration in Science and Philosophy. Boston, MA. Houghton Mifflin Company.

_____Nahin, P.J. (1998). An Imaginary Tale: The Story of $\sqrt{-1}$ Princeton, New Jersey. Princeton University Press.

_____Rigde, J.S. (2002). Hydrogen: The Essential Element. Cambridge, Mass. Harvard University Press.

_____Rovelli, C. (2014). Reality is Not What It Seems: The Journey to Quantum Gravity. New York, N.Y. Riverhead Books.

_____Rovelli, C. (2016). *Seven Brief Lessons on Physics.* New York, N.Y. Riverhead Books.

_____Rovelli, C. (2018). *The Order of Time.* New York, N.Y. Riverhead Books.

_____Rucker, R. (1982). Infinity and the Mind: The Science and Philosophy of the Infinite . Boston, MA. Birkhauser Publisher.

_____Sabbagh, K. (2003). The Rieman Hypothesis: The Greatest Unsolved Problem in Mathematics. New York, NY. Farrar, Strauss, and Groux.

_____Santoy M. (2003). The Music of the Primes: Searching to Solve the Greatest Mystery in Mathematics. New York. Harper Collins Publishers.

_____Singh S. (1997). Fermat's Enigma: The Epic Quest to Solve the World's Greatest Mathematical Problems. New York, NY. Anchor Books.

_____Toomey D. (2007). The New Time Traveler: A Journey to the Frontiers of Physics. New York. Norton and Company, Inc.

_____Trudeau, R.J. (1993). Introduction to Graph Theory. New York, Dover Publications.

_____Beckmann, P. (1993) A History of Pi. New York, Barnes, and Nobles.

_____Born, M. ((1962). Einstein's Theory of Relativity. New York, N.Y. Dover Publications, Inc.

_____Dirac, P.A.M. (2001). Lectures on Quantum Mechanics. Mineola, NY. Dover Publication, Inc.

_____Hemenway, P. (2005) Divine Proportion: Phi in Art, Nature, and Science. New York, NY. Sterling Publishing Company.

_____Levin, J. (2002). How the Universe Got Its Spots: Diary of a Finite Time in a Finite Space. Princeton, N.J. Princeton University Press.

_____Maor, E. (1994). e: The Story of Numbers. Princeton, New Jersey. Princeton University Press.

_____Ore, Oystein. (1988). Number Theory and Its History. New York. Dover Edition.

_____Tesla, N. (2007), My Inventions: The Autobiography of Nikola Tesla. Sioux, South Dakota. Nu Vision Publications, LLC.

_____Tesla, N. (1993). The Fantastic Inventions of Nicola Tesla. Kempton, Illinois, Adventure Unlimited Press.

_____Ouakninb, M.A. (2004) The Mystery of Numbers. New York, NY. Assouline Publishing.

_____Richeson, D.S. (2008) Euler's Gem: The Polyhedron Formula and the Birth of Topology. Princeton, N.J. Princeton University Press.

_____Connor, J.A. (2004) Kepler's Witch. An Astronomer's Discovery of Cosmic Order. Amid, Religious War, Political Intrigue, and the Heresy Trial of his Mother. New York, NY. Harper Collins Books.

_____Steinhardt, P.J. and Turok, N. (2007) Endless Universe: Beyond the Big Bang. New York, N.Y. Random House, Inc.

_____Shesso, R. (2007). Math for Mystics From the Fibonacci Sequence to Luna's Labyrinth to the Golden Section and other Secrets of Sacred Geometry. Newburyport, MA. Red Wheel Weiser Books.

_____Lawden, D.F. (2005) The Mathematical Principles of Quantum Mechanics. Mineola, NY Dover Publication, Inc.

_____Cox, B. and Forshaw, J. (2009)Why does E=m2 and (Why should we care). Philadelphia, PA. Da Capo Press.

_____Greene, B. (2005) The Fabric of the Cosmos; Space, Time, and the Texture of Reality. New York, NY. Vintage books Edition.

_____Adams F. and Laughlin, G. (2000). The Five Ages of the Universe. New York, NY. Touchstone First Edition.

_____Kaku, M. (2008). Physics of the Impossible: A Scientific Exploration Into the World of Phasers, Force Fields, Teleportation, and Time Travel. New York, NY. Doubleday.

_____Cole, K.C. (2003) Mind Over Matter: Conversation with the Cosmos. Orlando, Florida. Harcourt Books.

_____Morris, R. (2002). The Big Questions, Probing the Promise and Limits of Science. New York, N.Y. Holt, and Company.

--------Devlin, K. (2004). The Millenium Problems: The Seven Greatest Unsolved Mathematical Puzzles of Our Time. London. Granta Books.

_____Gullen, M. (1995) Five Equations the Changed the World: The Power and Poetry of Mathematics. New York, NY.LMJF Books.

_____Olsen S. (2006) The Golden Section: Nature Greatest Secret. New York. Walker Publishing Company

METHAPHYSICS/PHILOSOPHY

West, John A. (1987). *Serpent in the Sky. The High Wisdom of Ancient Egypt.* New York. The Julian Press.

ANCIENT MYISTERIES/SPIRITUALITY/NEW SCIENCE

_____Calleman, C.J. (2016) The Nine Waves of Creations: Quantum Physics, Holographic Evolution, and the Destiny of Humanity. Rochester, Vermont.. Bear and Company.

_____Heath, R. (2018) The Harmonic Origins of the World: Sacred Number at the Source of Creation. Rochester, Vermont. Inner Traditions.

_____Heindel, M. (2011). The Rosicrucian Cosmo Conception. Seattle, WA. Pacific Publishing Studio.

_____Holmes, E.(1988). The Science of Mind -50th Anniversary Edition. New York, NY. G.P. Putnam's Sons.

_____Mitchell, J. and Brown, A. ((2009) How the World is Made: The Story of Creation According to Sacred Geometry. Rochester, Vermont. Inner Traditions.

_____Russell, W. (1994), The Secret of Light. Waynesboro, Virginia. University of Science and Philosophy.

_____Foundation for Inner Peace. (1996) A Course in Miracles. Combined Volume Second Edition. New York, NY. Penguin Books USA.

_____Nozedar, A. (2008). The Illustrated Signs & Symbols Sourcebook. New York, N.Y. Metro Books.

The Author's Note

Born in Cuba, I believed I was Cuban.
Then I came to the United States, to New York.
Next, my ethnicity became Hispanic or Latino.
Later, I became a U.S. citizen.
I realized I was Cuban-American.
At that point, nationality faded away…
I felt free. I *am* free.
And so, I became a *Universal Citizen.*

With this journey of personal identity in mind, let me introduce myself to you, the reader. Professionally, I hold a master's degree in social work. Personally, I am a first-time author. Initially, I set out to write poetry and prose. However, my writing journey took an unexpected turn, leading me into the realm of personal growth and self-discovery.

The purpose of this book is to help readers to *consciously* explore the connection between the mind, body, spirit, God, and the Universe. Another central idea is that *you, I, and all of us are not separate beings.* We are all part of a single collective entity: *the Human Spirit.* At some point in our fragile lives, we must come to consciously understand this truth.

I challenge you, the reader, to examine your beliefs and habitual thoughts by asking yourself two essential questions:

1. What occupies your mind most of the time?

2. What are your greatest worries and fears?

Answering these questions with *awareness* marks the beginning of self-discovery. It is not an easy path, but with patience, discipline, and sincere intention and desire, it is possible!

If even one reader embarks on this journey, I will be fulfilled. If more than one does, my purpose in life will have been accomplished.

Thank you for reading.

Your Universal Citizen

To get in touch with the author:

Email: writers@thoughtsbymarlene.com

www.ingramcontent.com/pod-product-compliance
Lightning Source LLC
Chambersburg PA
CBHW051516120626
46551CB00012B/955